Young Frederick Douglass

FIGHT FOR FREEDOM

Young Frederick Douglass

FIGHT FOR FREEDOM

by Laurence Santrey
illustrated by Bert Dodson

Troll Associates

Library of Congress Cataloging in Publication Data

Santrey, Laurence.
   Young Frederick Douglass, fight for freedom.

   Summary: Presents the early life of the slave who
became an abolitionist, journalist, and statesman.
   1. Douglass, Frederick, 1817?-1895—Juvenile literature.   2. Abolitionists—United States—Biography—
Juvenile literature.   3. Afro-Americans—Biography—
Juvenile literature.   [1. Douglass, Frederick, 1817?-
1895.   2. Afro-Americans—Biography]   I. Dodson, Bert,
ill.   II. Title.
E449.D75S26   1983   973.8'092'4   [B]   [92]   82-15993
ISBN 0-89375-857-4
ISBN 0-89375-858-2 (pbk.)

10   9   8   7   6   5   4   3   2

Young Frederick Douglass

FIGHT FOR FREEDOM

Fred Baily's world was bleak and poor. The little boy didn't know it, though, for Betsey and Isaac Baily, his grandparents, were kind and loving people. They took good care of Fred and his young cousins.

The children lived with Grandmama and Grandpapa because their mothers were not allowed to keep them. Their mothers— Grandmama Baily's daughters—were slaves who worked on different plantations on the eastern shore of Maryland. When one of them had a baby, Grandmama Baily took it in. She raised the child until it was old enough to be put to work by its slave owner.

Fred, who was born about 1817, was better off than a lot of other slave children. Many of them had no relatives like Grandmama Baily to care for them. Those children were raised by strangers, who did not treat them well. But Fred's grandmother made sure that her little ones had enough food and plenty of affection, and that they never felt lonely or frightened.

Betsey Baily was smart and skilled in many ways. One of her special talents was farming. Her sweet potatoes grew bigger and better—and there were more of them—than anyone else's in the whole area. The neighbors said she was "born to good luck." But, as Fred wrote years later, Grandmama's secret wasn't luck. It was the special care and attention she gave to her seedlings.

To keep her sweet-potato seedlings from being destroyed by frost, she actually buried the roots under the hearth of her cabin during the winter months. Then, when they were planted, they were healthy and grew well. Whenever the neighbors had seedlings to put in the ground, they sent for Grandmama Betsey. "If she but touches them at planting," the neighbors believed, "they will be sure to grow and flourish." For lending her magic touch, Mrs. Baily was always given a share of the crop. And that brought more food into the Baily cabin.

For the first few years of his life, Fred never saw his mother. He didn't even *know* what a mother was. As for his father—the idea of such a person never entered his mind. If Fred belonged to anyone, it was to his master.

Little Fred spent his days playing with his cousins, helping his grandmother, or fishing in the river near the cabin. His only clothing was a rough, knee-length shirt. A slave child was given two shirts each year. Even if these shirts were torn or lost, there were no new ones until the year was up. Long after, Fred remembered, "In the hottest summer and the coldest winter, I was kept almost naked. No shoes, no stockings, no jacket, no trousers. Nothing but the coarse shirt reaching down to my knees. This I wore night and day, changing it once a week."

Until he was around five years old, Fred didn't know he was a slave. Then he heard his grandparents talking about the "Old Master," who owned all of Fred's family. There was a sad note in Grandmama Betsey's voice when she spoke about the plantation, where Fred would soon have to go. The little boy didn't understand much of what they were saying, but the sound of it made him shiver.

Nothing happened for two years. Then, one summer morning, Betsey Baily took her grandson's hand and set off along the road. She didn't tell him where they were going, or why. She didn't cry or show any of the gloom she was feeling. Not once on the twelve-mile walk to the plantation house did she speak one sad word. Yet somehow, Fred sensed that something terrible was happening.

In the blazing afternoon heat, Mrs. Baily and Fred reached the plantation. The little boy saw many houses, farm animals, men, women, and children. All of this stunned him. Living at Grandmama's, he had never seen so many buildings and people all in one place.

Mrs. Baily brought Fred over to a young boy and two young girls. "Fred," she said, "here is your brother, Perry. And these are your sisters, Sarah and Eliza. You run along and play with them. I'll sit in the kitchen and visit awhile."

Fred was confused and trembling. The children

might be called brother and sisters, but they were strangers to him. He clung tightly to Grandmama's skirt. He wanted to go home.

Grandmama insisted that Fred stay outside and play. She gave him a gentle push toward the other children. Then she walked away. Fred stood there, watching the other children play. Time passed, but he didn't budge from the spot. Then a child ran over to him, saying, "Your grand-mammy's gone." Fred couldn't believe it. He dashed into the house to see for himself. It *was* true! Grandmama Betsey was gone.

The heart-broken boy threw himself on the floor and sobbed. His brother and sisters tried to comfort him, but nothing could stop his tears. Fred felt betrayed, terrified, and all alone. Now he suddenly understood what his grandparents had been talking about and why they had been so sad. Lying on the dirt floor, Fred cried himself to sleep.

For the next two years, Fred lived on the plantation as the slave of a man named Captain Anthony. Fred was still too young to work in the fields, so he was given other chores. He helped the older boys bring in the cows for milking. He kept the front yard clean. He ran errands for Captain Anthony's family.

Even though the work wasn't too difficult, Fred was always hungry and tired. Slaves were awakened long before sunrise and kept busy until long after dark. Breakfast for the slave children was cornmeal mush. It was dumped into a large wooden bowl on the ground. All the children squatted around the bowl to eat, scooping up the mush with oyster shells, flat stones, or their fingers.

The strongest children and the fastest eaters got the most food. But *nobody* ever had enough food. Little Fred got the least of all because Aunt Katy, the cook, was his enemy.

One morning, Katy threatened to starve the life out of Fred. All day, he tried to keep up his spirits, hoping she would forget by dinnertime. But she didn't. At sundown, she gave each of the children dinner—one slice of corn bread. When Fred reached for his, she pulled away the loaf and sent him out of the kitchen.

The eight-year-old boy, too hungry to fall asleep that night, was sitting outside the kitchen door when he had a surprise visitor. It was his mother. Harriet Baily was almost a stranger to Fred. Since he had come to the plantation, he had seen her only three times.

Fred's mother was a slave on a farm fifteen miles away. The only way she could visit her children was to walk thirty miles at night. Her long, hard day in the fields left her too tired for that kind of walk. This time, however, she was able to get a ride on a cart.

Harriet Baily put her arm around Fred and asked him how he was. He told her he was hungry and that the cook had threatened to starve him to death. The woman kissed her son, stroked his cheek, and said, "I won't let anyone starve you!" Then she gave him a heart-shaped ginger cake coated with sugar.

23

As soon as Fred finished the last crumb, his mother took him into the kitchen. In a voice filled with fury, she told Aunt Katy, "You're a slave just like the rest of us. How can you do these things to a harmless little child?"

Harriet Baily's angry words didn't change Katy's treatment of Fred. But his mother's visit still made a big difference in the young boy's life. "That night," he remembered, "I learned that I was not only a child, but *somebody's* child." He knew that his mother loved him very much, and even though she couldn't be with him, she thought of him all the time. But after that night, Fred never saw Harriet Baily again. She died when Fred was only eight or nine years old.

Before he was ten years old, Fred was sent to the city of Baltimore. He was going to work for Sophia and Hugh Auld, relatives of Captain Anthony. The young boy was glad to leave the plantation. He felt that whatever lay ahead could not be worse.

On a sunny Saturday morning in spring, Fred
was dressed in a clean shirt and his first pair of
pants. He was put aboard a sloop bound for
Baltimore—a trip he never forgot. He gaped at the
broad Chesapeake Bay and all the boats sailing on
it. He marveled at the town of Annapolis, with its

beautiful houses and the great shining dome of the State House. But most exciting of all was Baltimore itself, a city teeming with life. For the youngster who had never been away from the country, this was a fantasyland.

One of the sailors took Fred to the Auld house. Fred was met at the door by Mr. and Mrs. Auld and their little son, Tommy. Fred knew he was going to live with them and take care of Tommy. He didn't know how he was going to be treated. But when little Tommy smiled and took his hand, the young slave could see that fate had been kind to him.

Instead of sleeping on the ground, Fred now slept indoors on a bed of straw. He had clean clothes and enough food to fill his belly. Nobody beat him, and Mrs. Auld treated him like an ordinary child instead of a slave.

Every afternoon, when Fred brought Tommy home from play, the boys joined Mrs. Auld in the front parlor. There they sat quietly, listening to her read from the Bible.

Fred loved to hear Mrs. Auld read aloud. He enjoyed the sounds of the words and the wonderful stories they made. He wished he could read them, too. And so, one day, he asked Mrs. Auld if she would teach him to read. "Why, how nice, Fred," she said. "It's delightful that you want to read the Bible. Of course, I'll teach you. We shall start with the alphabet this very afternoon!"

In the days that followed, Mrs. Auld gave Fred a reading lesson every afternoon. Soon the young slave knew the alphabet and could spell many short words. Fred looked forward to each afternoon's lesson with great excitement and was very proud when Mrs. Auld praised him for being so bright. He had never known such joy.

One evening, Mrs. Auld told her husband how well Fred was learning to read. Mr. Auld scowled. "You must stop these lessons right now!" he told his wife. "Don't you know that it is against the law to teach slaves to read? It's a bad thing to do."

"I didn't know it was against the law," Mrs. Auld answered. "And I cannot understand why it would be bad for a slave to read."

"A slave should know nothing but the will of his master," Mr. Auld explained. "If you teach that boy how to read, he'll be forever unfit for the duties of a slave. The knowledge will do him no good, and it will do us a great deal of harm."

Mrs. Auld never gave Fred another lesson. In fact, she did everything possible to stop him from learning. If she saw the boy looking at a newspaper or book, she snatched it away. And if she didn't see or hear him doing some task, she accused him of sneaking off somewhere to read.

Life changed for Mrs. Auld, too. She was obeying the law and her husband. She was being a good slave owner. But she was no longer a happy woman.

Fred was hurt deeply by what had happened, but he learned two valuable lessons. First, he realized that his owners wanted him to be a slave forever. He understood now that people were not slaves because of something they did. They were slaves because somebody else wanted them to be.

The second lesson was that the way out of slavery was through knowledge. That was why slave owners kept their slaves ignorant. Once slaves could read road signs, they might run away from their masters. Once they found out that there were states without slavery, they might try to reach them. Once they learned to write, they could forge the papers slaves needed to travel. And once they could count, they could use money to buy train tickets and food.

Young Fred Baily made up his mind to learn how to read and write. First, he read everything he could from a spelling book someone had thrown away. Whenever he came to a word he didn't know, he made a small mark under it and asked one of the neighborhood children to tell him what it was. Fred paid for these brief lessons with cookies from the Auld kitchen. By the time he was thirteen, Fred could read very well.

About the same time, Fred began working in the shipyard owned by Mr. Auld. His job was to clean up, watch the yard when nobody else was around, and keep the office fire going. There were many hours when he was alone, and Fred used them to teach himself to write.

One day, he found a school notebook Tommy Auld had finished using. In the spaces between the lines, Fred copied Tommy's writing. He worked in the kitchen by firelight, waiting until the Auld family was fast asleep.

Then in March 1833, Fred was sent back to the plantation. There was a big argument in the Auld family between Hugh Auld and his brother, Thomas. As a result, Hugh had to return Fred to the country.

Thomas Auld, Fred's new master, treated his slaves badly. Yet, no matter how many hardships he had to endure, Fred refused to beg or weep or show any other sign that it bothered him. This made Thomas Auld so furious that he sent Fred away to be "broken."

On January 1, 1834, Fred was brought to the farm of Edward Covey. For a fee, Covey promised that he would turn "trouble-making" slaves into obedient workers.

For the first six months, Fred took everything Covey handed out. But one day, when Covey was beating Fred, the seventeen-year-old slave fought back. Fred won the fight, knocking Covey to the ground. The enraged slave breaker swore he would kill Fred. But the teenager knew better. Covey would not do anything that would cost him his fee.

From that moment until Fred left Covey's, the young slave was never whipped, nor did Covey ever again challenge him. Years later, Fred wrote, "This battle with Mr. Covey was the turning point in my life as a slave. It rekindled in me the smoldering embers of liberty. I was a changed being after that fight. I was *nothing* before; *I was a man now*. It inspired me with a renewed determination to be *a free man!*"

After three years of farm work in the country, Fred was sent back to Baltimore. There, Hugh Auld got him a job in a friend's shipyard. Fred liked the work—he was a skilled laborer now—and he was happier in Baltimore than he had been in the country. But there was one important thing still missing—his freedom! Then he met a man who offered him a way to escape slavery.

The man was a black sailor who had seaman's papers. These papers, issued by the United States government, proved that the sailor was not a slave. With them, he was free to travel anywhere in the country. The sailor offered to lend Fred his papers. "Put these in your pocket," he said, "and you can go North to freedom. You can mail them back to me when you're safe in New York or Boston."

On September 3, 1838, wearing sailor's clothing and carrying his friend's papers, Fred Baily got on a northbound train. He didn't stop until he reached New Bedford, Massachusetts, a ship-building town. There, Fred took a job in a shipyard, married Anna Murray, a free black woman from Baltimore, and started a new life.

It was in New Bedford that Fred took the last name of Douglass. As Fred Baily, he might be traced by bounty hunters who were paid for turning in runaway slaves. With a new name, Frederick Douglass, he had a much better chance of staying free.

It was also in New Bedford that Fred began the career that would make him world famous. He started by joining a group of abolitionists, people devoted to ending slavery. He read everything he could about slavery and listened to the leading abolitionists of his day. Then, in 1841, Frederick Douglass made his first anti-slavery speech. It thrilled his audience, and it brought him to the attention of every important person in the abolitionist movement.

For the next four years, Frederick Douglass toured the Northern states, speaking against slavery. He also wrote the story of his life. The book, which described his years as a slave, was read all over the United States. It was even read by the Auld family, who grew very angry. They went to court to have their runaway slave returned to them.

Douglass's friends were afraid that he would be arrested and sent back to Maryland, so they put him on a ship bound for England. He stayed in England for two years and became a very popular speaker and writer. But he wanted to come home, where he felt a strong voice against slavery was needed more than ever. To make this possible, his friends raised enough money to buy Douglass's freedom from the Aulds.

When he returned to the United States in the years before the Civil War, Frederick Douglass continued his work for freedom. He started a weekly newspaper in Rochester, New York called *The North Star*. This paper soon became a leading force in the battle against slavery.

Shortly after the war began, Douglass went to see President Abraham Lincoln. He urged the President to recruit black men, as well as white, into the Union Army.

"Why do you fight the rebels with only one hand," Douglass asked, "when you might strike effectively with two?"

Lincoln agreed. Within months, thousands of black men were fighting for the Union. Among them were two of Frederick Douglass's sons.

Even though the Civil War ended slavery, many problems remained for black people. They still did not have equal rights. In many places, they could not vote, hold public office, find jobs, or get an education. And so, Douglass continued his battle for civil rights and freedom. He fought tirelessly for an end to job discrimination and to the segregation in schools and places of worship.

Frederick Douglass did not stop fighting until his death on February 20, 1895. Yet, even though he is gone, his beliefs are still alive today. Douglass's words continue to live, showing others the path to freedom and equality for *all* people.

Patterns and Themes

A Basic English Reader

Third Edition

Judy R. Rogers ~ Glenn C. Rogers

Morehead State University, Kentucky

Patterns and Themes

A Basic English Reader

Third Edition

Wadsworth Publishing Company

A Division of Wadsworth, Inc.

Belmont, California

English Editor: *Angela Gantner*
Editorial Assistant: *Tricia Schumacher*
Production Editor: *Donna Linden*
Designer: *Cloyce Wall*
Print Buyer: *Barbara Britton*
Permissions Editor: *Jeanne Bosschart*
Copy Editor: *Robert Fiske*
Cover Designer: *Roger Knox*
Signing Representative: *Mark Francisco*
Compositor: *TypeLink, Inc., San Diego, California*
Printer: *Malloy Lithographing, Ann Arbor, Michigan*
Acknowledgments appear on pages 239 and 240.

 This book is printed on acid-free recycled paper.

Printed in the United States of America

4 5 6 7 8 9 10—97 96 95 94

Library of Congress Cataloging-in-Publication Data

Patterns and themes : a basic English reader / [compiled
    by] Judy R. Rogers, Glenn C. Rogers.—3rd ed.
        p. cm.
    ISBN 0-534-17988-6 (alk. paper)
    1. College readers.   2. English language—
    Rhetoric.   3. Basic English.   I. Rogers,
    Judy R.   II. Rogers, Glenn C.
PE1417.P358   1993
808'.0427—dc20   92-20560

Thematic Table of Contents

Laughter

Differences

Sports

Work

Heroism

Women and Men

The Environment

Frontiers

Rhetorical Table of Contents

Description

Narration

Illustration

Definition

Comparison/Contrast

Analysis

Cause and Effect

Persuasion

For John and James
who encourage us for their own reasons

Preface

Patterns and Themes is a collection of readings and writing assignments especially for students enrolled in basic or developmental writing courses. This edition of *Patterns and Themes* continues to provide brief readings selected to stimulate interest and reinforce frequently used writing patterns. As in earlier editions, the content of the selections will appeal to college readers, but the readability level is comfortable for basic writing students. This edition contains eighteen new selections by experienced writers and two new student essays.

Arrangement of the Text   The selections are grouped, first of all, by theme. For many students, especially those not ready to study rhetorical patterns, this arrangement provides a natural way to integrate material. To freshen the text for continuing users, there are two changes in themes from the second edition.

The themes are common to large groups of people from diverse backgrounds, and thus we have been able to represent varying points of view on the same topic. We hope those who use this text will learn more about themselves and others: the same essay may be a mirror for one reader and a window for another.

The selections in this edition maintain the variety of the earlier editions: sketches, short stories, popular and academic nonfiction, journalism, student essays, and a brief narrative poem. These readings are variously entertaining, informative, persuasive, thought provoking.

Over the years, amid the rapids and eddies of changing composition theory, many writing teachers have continued to have success introducing their students to rhetorical forms. Thus, in an alternate table of contents, we have indicated the common rhetorical tools used by the writers included in *Patterns and Themes*. Basic writers generally understand and move naturally toward uncomplicated organizational patterns. Therefore, we have chosen a number of examples of narration and description, often of personal experiences. But we have also included selections that exhibit development by other frequently used rhetorical modes. In this edition, there is an increased emphasis on persuasive writing because it stimulates analytical thinking and encourages students to become more sensitive to the daily barrage of persuasion in its many forms.

Aids to Reading and Writing   To increase students' enjoyment of the material and to speed the development of their reading and writing skills, we have included several learning aids. "Looking Forward" gives brief biographical information about the authors (when relevant) and points students toward main ideas and important writing strategies. "Help with Words" offers short definitions, often contextual, of many words that may be unfamiliar. "A Second Look" sends students back to selections to consider points of meaning and to look again at writing techniques. Sometimes students are asked to consider ideas from two or more of the selections within a unit, thereby increasing their awareness of thematic unity and differing writing techniques.

"Ideas for Writing" suggests writing assignments for paragraphs and, more often, short essays. In the early units, the emphasis is on description and narration. Later assignments—like later reading selections—increase in difficulty and introduce definition, comparison/contrast, process, persuasion, and reports using outside sources. Realizing that basic writers advance at different rates, we continue to suggest topics for description and narration throughout. Many of the assignments are structured to help students move through the writing process, especially the prewriting or planning stage. Instructors may easily substitute their own topics while still following the suggestions for prewriting.

"Making Connections" helps develop students' critical thinking skills while suggesting the thematic links within a unit. The questions and suggestions in "Making Connections" call upon students to compare, contrast, define, evaluate, identify values, recognize stereotypes, identify key issues, and perform other basic critical thinking tasks. These suggestions can lead to class or small group discussion or to writing assignments.

Rationale of *Patterns and Themes*   This text originally grew out of our discontent with basic writing courses that were given almost exclusively to drill and practice. Basic writing instruction has changed considerably in the intervening years, but many teachers still find a need for sentence-combining exercises, grammar drills, and punctuation lessons. These assignments may be helpful, even essential; but, unleavened by other material, they frequently become tedious to students and instructors alike. Reading, group discussion, and varied writing tasks add interest to basic composition, helping students build skills more rapidly.

As in the first and second editions of *Patterns and Themes*, we acknowledge the pioneering work of Mina Shaughnessy who, in *Errors and Expecta-*

tions, argues for integrated instruction in writing and reading. Her ideas, and those of many others, have helped to shape all three editions of this text. We hope that every student who uses this book will become the student Shaughnessy describes: "a more careful writer and a more critical reader."

Acknowledgments   We wish to thank the reviewers who offered their suggestions for improving this edition: William Cooper, Jr., Allan Hancock College; David Denny, De Anza College; Timothy A. Miank, Lansing Community College; and Violet M. O'Valle, Tarrant County Junior College, South Campus. We especially appreciate the thoughtful comments of John L. Coble, San Bernardino Valley College, and Linda Daigle, Houston Community College, who have used *Patterns and Themes* before and who offered practical and encouraging advice for improving the current edition. As before, we have benefitted from the counsel of Angie Gantner, Donna Linden, and other members of the Wadsworth staff. Finally, a word of appreciation to Caroline Hensley who once more proved invaluable.

Patterns and Themes

A Basic English Reader

Third Edition

Memories

Salvation

Langston Hughes

Looking Forward

Langston Hughes—playwright, poet, fiction writer, expert in jazz and folklore—was one of the most influential figures in the history of African-American literature. In "Salvation," a section of his autobiography, Hughes recalls an experience from his youth that left him sad and disappointed. As you read, remember that a piece of writing should introduce and develop a main idea or central point. Hughes's main idea is introduced early. Watch for its development.

 Help with Words

fold *(paragraph 1):* a pen for sheep; here, a church or its congregation
escorted *(paragraph 1):* accompanied or led
rhythmical *(paragraph 3):* with regular accents or beats
dire *(paragraph 3):* dreadful
work-gnarled *(paragraph 4):* roughened or hardened from work
rounder *(paragraph 6):* a drunkard
serenely *(paragraph 7):* peacefully
knickerbockered *(paragraph 11):* wearing knickerbockers: short pants gathered at the knee
ecstatic *(paragraph 14):* greatly joyful, delighted

I was saved from sin when I was going on thirteen. But not 1 really saved. It happened like this. There was a big revival at my Auntie Reed's church. Every night for weeks there had been much preaching, singing, praying, and shouting, and some very hardened sinners had been brought to Christ, and the membership of the church had grown by leaps and bounds. Then just before the revival ended, they held a special meeting for children, "to bring the young lambs to the fold." My aunt spoke of it for days ahead. That night I was escorted to the front row and placed on the mourners' bench with all the other young sinners, who had not yet been brought to Jesus.

My aunt told me that when you were saved you saw a light, and something happened to you inside! And Jesus came into your life! And God was with you from then on! She said you could see and hear and feel Jesus in your soul. I believed her. I had heard a great many old people say the same thing and it seemed to me they ought to know. So I sat there calmly in the hot crowded church, waiting for Jesus to come to me.   2

The preacher preached a wonderful rhythmical sermon, all moans and shouts and lonely cries and dire pictures of hell, and then he sang a song about the ninety and nine safe in the fold, but one little lamb was left in the cold. Then he said, "Won't you come? Won't you come to Jesus? Young lambs, won't you come?" And he held out his arms to all us young sinners there on the mourners' bench. And the little girls cried. And some of them jumped up and went to Jesus right away. But most of us just sat there.   3

A great many old people came and knelt around us and prayed, old women with jet-black faces and braided hair, old men with work-gnarled hands. And the church sang a song about the lower lights are burning, some poor sinners to be saved. And the whole building rocked with prayer and song.   4

Still I kept waiting to see Jesus.   5

Finally all the young people had gone to the altar and were saved, but one boy and me. He was a rounder's son named Westley. Westley and I were surrounded by sisters and deacons praying. It was very hot in the church, and getting late now. Finally Westley said to me in a whisper: "Goddamn! I'm tired o' sitting here. Let's get up and be saved." So he got up and was saved.   6

Then I was left all alone on the mourners' bench. My aunt came and knelt at my knees and cried, while prayers and songs swirled all around me in the little church. The whole congregation prayed for me alone, in a mighty wail of moans and voices. And I kept waiting serenely for Jesus, waiting, waiting—but he didn't come. I wanted to see him, but nothing happened to me. Nothing! I wanted something to happen to me, but nothing happened.   7

I heard the songs and the minister saying: "Why don't you come? 8
My dear child, why don't you come to Jesus? Jesus is waiting for
you. He wants you. Why don't you come? Sister Reed, what is this
child's name?"

"Langston," my aunt sobbed. 9

"Langston, why don't you come? Why don't you come and be 10
saved? Oh, Lamb of God! Why don't you come?"

Now it was really getting late. I began to be ashamed of myself, 11
holding everything up so long. I began to wonder what God
thought about Westley, who certainly hadn't seen Jesus either, but
who was now sitting proudly on the platform, swinging his knickerbockered legs and grinning down at me, surrounded by deacons
and old women on their knees praying. God had not struck Westley
dead for taking his name in vain or for lying in the temple. So I
decided that maybe to save further trouble, I'd better lie, too, and
say that Jesus had come, and get up and be saved.

So I got up.   •   12

Suddenly the whole room broke into a sea of shouting, as they 13
saw me rise. Waves of rejoicing swept the place. Women leaped into
the air. My aunt threw her arms around me. The minister took me
by the hand and led me to the platform.

When things quieted down, in a hushed silence, punctuated by a 14
few ecstatic "Amens," all the new young lambs were blessed in the
name of God. Then joyous singing filled the room.

That night, for the last time in my life but one—for I was a big boy 15
twelve years old—I cried. I cried, in bed alone, and couldn't stop. I
buried my head under the quilts, but my aunt heard me. She woke
up and told my uncle I was crying because the Holy Ghost had
come into my life, and because I had seen Jesus. But I was really
crying because I couldn't bear to tell her that I had lied, that I had
deceived everybody in the church, and I hadn't seen Jesus, and that
now I didn't believe there was a Jesus any more, since he didn't
come to help me.

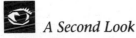 *A Second Look*

1 Pick out some descriptive words in paragraphs 3 and 4 that help you
picture the scene in the church.

2 Hughes uses time order to organize his narrative. Transitional words at the beginnings of paragraphs emphasize this pattern. Locate these linking words at the beginning of paragraphs 5, 6, and 7. Are other paragraphs linked in this way?

3 Although writers usually avoid using one-sentence paragraphs except in reproducing speech, Hughes uses two (paragraphs 5 and 12). What does he achieve by doing this?

4 Why does young Hughes pretend to feel something that he has not really experienced?

5 Read the last paragraph again and state, in one sentence, why Hughes is crying.

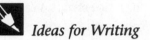 *Ideas for Writing*

Describe for a group of classmates something that happened to you when you were younger that left you frustrated or disappointed. Make sure your readers understand first what you expected to happen and then what actually happened.

After you choose the incident, write down everything you can remember about it. Do not worry about the order of your ideas or the mechanics of your writing. Just get your thoughts on paper. Then read through what you have written and select the details that seem most interesting and important. Mark these details so that you can refer to them later.

Next, decide how you will begin telling about your experience. Write the opening. Then continue describing the experience, using the details you have marked, until you reach the end. Your closing may explain why the incident was important. (Reread Hughes's last paragraph.)

Finally, reread your paper to see whether it says exactly what you want it to say. Make sure that the ideas are clear and that the details support the main idea.

The Woman Warrior

Maxine Hong Kingston

Looking Forward

Maxine Hong Kingston, born in California to Chinese parents, has become one of the most important of the modern Chinese American writers. She is the author of several books as well as a teacher of creative writing. In her autobiography, *The Woman Warrior*, Kingston recalls how, in her girlhood, she was caught between two cultures—the old one of China, which she had never seen, and the new one of America, which her family had not completely joined. In this selection, we see her growing rebellion against the harshly antifeminist attitudes of the emigrant Chinese.

 ### *Help with Words*

emigrant *(paragraph 5):* a person who has left one region or country to move to another

talking-story *(paragraph 11):* telling a story

grievances *(paragraph 12):* complaints

outward tendency *(paragraph 18):* refers to the usual custom among Chinese girls of leaving their families and becoming part of their husbands' families

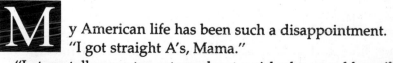

My American life has been such a disappointment.   1

"I got straight A's, Mama."   2

"Let me tell you a true story about a girl who saved her village."   3

I could not figure out what was my village. And it was important   4
that I do something big and fine, or else my parents would sell me

when we made our way back to China. In China there were solutions for what to do with little girls who ate up food and threw tantrums. You can't eat straight A's.

When one of my parents or the emigrant villagers said, "Feeding girls is feeding cowbirds," I would thrash on the floor and scream so hard I couldn't talk. I couldn't stop.   5

"What's the matter with her?"   6

"I don't know. Bad, I guess. You know how girls are. 'There's no profit in raising girls. Better to raise geese than girls.'"   7

"I would hit her if she were mine. But then there's no use wasting all that discipline on a girl. 'When you raise girls, you're raising children for strangers.'"   8

"Stop that crying!" my mother would yell. "I'm going to hit you if you don't stop. Bad girl! Stop!" I'm going to remember never to hit or to scold my children for crying, I thought, because then they will only cry more.   9

"I'm not a bad girl," I would scream. "I'm not a bad girl. I'm not a bad girl." I might as well have said, "I'm not a girl."   10

"When you were little, all you had to say was 'I'm not a bad girl,' and you could make yourself cry," my mother says, talking-story about my childhood.   11

I minded that the emigrant villagers shook their heads at my sister and me. "One girl—and another girl," they said, and made our parents ashamed to take us out together. The good part about my brothers being born was that people stopped saying, "All girls," but I learned new grievances. "Did you roll an egg on my face like that when I was born?" "Did you have a full-month party for me?" "Did you turn on all the lights?" "Did you send my picture to Grandmother?" "Why not? Because I'm a girl? Is that why not?" "Why didn't you teach me English?" "You like having me beaten up at school, don't you?"   12

"She is very mean, isn't she?" the emigrant villagers would say.   13

"Come, children. Hurry. Hurry. Who wants to go out with Great-Uncle?" On Saturday mornings my great-uncle, the ex-river pirate, did the shopping. "Get your coats, whoever's coming."   14

"I'm coming. I'm coming. Wait for me."   15

When he heard girls' voices, he turned on us and roared, "No girls!" and left my sisters and me hanging our coats back up, not looking at one another. The boys came back with candy and new   16 toys. When they walked through Chinatown, the people must have said, "a boy—and another boy—and another boy!" At my great-uncle's funeral I secretly tested out feeling glad that he was dead—the six-foot bearish masculinity of him.

I went away to college—Berkeley in the sixties—and I studied, 17 and I marched to change the world, but I did not turn into a boy. I would have liked to bring myself back as a boy for my parents to welcome with chickens and pigs. That was for my brother, who returned alive from Vietnam.

If I went to Vietnam, I would not come back; females desert fami- 18 lies. It was said, "There is an outward tendency in females," which meant that I was getting straight A's for the good of my future husband's family, not my own. I did not plan ever to have a husband. I would show my mother and father and the nosey emigrant villagers that girls have no outward tendency. I stopped getting straight A's.

 A Second Look

1 Why is Kingston's family not impressed that young Maxine got straight A's?

2 Explain what Kingston means in paragraph 10.

3 What kinds of distinctions does the family make between sons and daughters?

4 In what ways does Kingston rebel against the culture that rejected her? Why does she choose the strategy she does?

Ideas for Writing

Have you ever been in serious disagreement with the attitudes and beliefs of your family? Write about this situation, telling your readers (a group of people your own age) what these beliefs were and describing how you rebelled against them. Your essay should give clear answers to these questions:

1 What were the beliefs you and your family disagreed over?

2 How did you and the family express your feelings? Give examples.

3 Were you able to settle these differences? If so, how? If not, what have been the results of your continued disagreement?

Down These Mean Streets

Piri Thomas

Looking Forward

Piri Thomas was born to Puerto Rican parents in Spanish Harlem. In his twenties, Thomas, a drug user, was imprisoned for attempted armed robbery. Cured of his addiction and released from prison, he became a drug rehabilitation worker in Spanish Harlem and Puerto Rico. In an early chapter of his autobiography, *Down These Mean Streets*, Thomas writes about his hatred of school and teachers. In this selection, he tells about one of his many conflicts in the classroom. Notice how this street-smart kid can turn a bad situation partly to his own advantage.

 Help with Words

muted *(paragraph 15):* quiet
Qué pasa? *(paragraph 17):* What's the matter? (Spanish)
chastised *(paragraph 20):* punished
intention *(paragraph 25):* wish, purpose
discretion *(paragraph 39):* caution
valor *(paragraph 39):* bravery
padre *(paragraph 41):* father (Spanish)
muchacho *(paragraph 43):* boy (Spanish)

O ne class I didn't dig at all was the so-called "Open Air 1 Class" for skinny, "underweight" kids. We had to sleep a couple of half hours every day, and we got extra milk and jelly and peanut butter on brown bread. The teacher, Miss Shepard, was like a dried-up grape. One day I raised my hand to go to the toilet, but she paid me no mind. After a while, the pain was getting bad, so I called out, "Miss Shepard, may I leave the room?"

She looked up and just shook her head, no. 2

"But I gotta go, Miss Shepard." 3

"You just went a little while ago," she said. 4

"I know, Miss Shepard, but I gotta go again." 5

"I think it's sheer nonsense," said the old bitch. "You just want an 6 excuse to play around in the hallways." . . .

I had to go so badly that I felt the tears forming in the corners of 7 my eyes to match the drops that were already making a wet scene down my leg. "I'm goin' anyway," I said, and started toward the door.

Miss Shepard got up and screamed at me to get back to my seat. I 8 ignored her.

"Get back to your seat, young man," she screamed. "Do you hear 9 me? Get right back—" . . .

I reached the door and felt her hands grab out at me and her 10 fingers hook on to the back of my shirt collar. My clean, washed-a-million-times shirt came apart in her hand.

I couldn't see her face clearly when I turned around. All I could 11 think about was my torn shirt and how this left me with only two others. All I could see was her being the cause of the dampness of my pants and hot pee running down my leg. All I could hear was the kids making laughing sounds and the anger of my being ashamed. I didn't think of her as a woman, but as something that had to be hit. I hit it. . . .

"You struck me! You *struck* me! Oh, help, help!" she cried. 12

I cut out. Man, I ran like hell into the hallway, and she came right 13 after me, yelling, "Help, help!" I was scared now and all I could think about was getting back to my Moms, my home, my block, where no one could hurt me. I ran toward the stairway and found it blocked off by a man, the principal. I cut back toward the back stairs.

"Stop him! Stop him!" dear Miss Shepard yelled, pointing her 14
finger at me. "He struck me, he struck me."

I looked over my shoulder and saw the principal talk to her for a 15
hot second and then take off after me, yelling: "Stop! Stop!" I hit the
stairs and went swooming down like it was all one big step. The
principal was fast and I could hear him swearing right behind me. I
slammed through the main-floor door that led to the lunchroom
and jumped over benches and tables, trying like hell to make the
principal trip and break a leg. Then I heard a muted cry of pain as a
bench caught him in the shin. I looked over my shoulder and I dug
his face. The look said that he was gonna hit me; that he wasn't
gonna listen to my side of the story; that I had no side. I figured I
better not get caught.

I busted my legs running toward the door that led to the outside 16
and freedom, and with both hands out in front of me I hit the brass
bar that opens the door. Behind me I heard a thump as the principal
smacked into it. I ran down the block, sneaking a look behind me.
The principal was right behind me, his face redder and meaner.
People were looking at the uneven contest.

I tore into my hallway, screaming as loud as I could for help. The 17
apartment doors opened up, one right after another. Heads of all
colors popped out. *"Qué pasa?"* asked a Puerto Rican woman.
"Wha's happenin'?" said a colored lady.

"They wanna beat me up in school and that's one of them," I 18
puffed, pointing at the principal, who was just coming into view.

"Hooo, ain't nobody gonna hurt you, sonny," said the colored 19
lady, whose name was Miss Washington. She gently pushed me
behind her with one hand and with the other held it out toward the
principal roaring down at us.

The principal, blocked by Miss Washington's 280 pounds and a 20
look of "Don't you touch that boy," stopped short and puffed out,
"That—that—kid—he—punched a teacher and—he's got to be
chastised for it. After all, school disci—"

"Now hol' on, white man," Miss Washington interrupted. "There 21
ain't nobody gonna chaz—whatever it is—this boy. I knows him
an' he's a good boy—at least good for what comes outta this heah
trashy neighborhood—an' you ain't gonna do nuttin' to him, unless
you-all wan's to walk over me."

Miss Washington was talking real bad-like. I peeked out from 22
behind that great behind.

"Madam, I assure you," the principal said, "I didn't mean harm-   23
ing him in a bodily manner. And if you knew the whole issue, you
would agree with me that he deserves being chastised. As principal
of his school, I have his best interest at heart. Ha, ha, ha," he added,
"you know the old saying, madam, 'A stitch in time saves nine.' Ha,
ha, ha—*ahurmph*."

I could see him putting that stitch in my head.   24

"I assure you, madam," he continued, smilingly pretty, "we have   25
no intention of doing him bodily harm."

Once again I peeked out from behind Miss Washington's behind.   26
"Yeah, that's what you say," I said. "How about alla time you take
kids down to your office for some crap and ya start poking 'em with
that big finger of yours until they can't take it anymore?"

There were a lot of people in the hall by this time. They were all   27
listening, and I knew it. "Yeah, ask any of the kids," I added.
"They'll tell ya." I looked sorry-like at the crowd of people, who
were now murmuring mean-like and looking at the principal like he
didn't have long on this earth.

Smelling a Harlem lynch party in the making, I said, "An'—   28
you—ain't—gonna—do—it—to—me. I'll get me a forty-five an'—"

"Hush you mouth, boy," Miss Washington said; "don't be talkin'   29
like that. We grownups will get this all straightened out. An' nobody's gonna poke no finger in your chest"—she looked dead at
the principal—"is they?"

The principal smiled the weakest smile in this smiling world.   30
"I—I—I—er, assure you, madam, this young man is gifted with the
most wonderful talent for prevarication I've ever seen."

"What's that mean?" Miss Washington asked suspiciously.   31

"Er, it means a good imagination, madam. A-ha-ha—yes,   32
ahurmph."

"That's a lie, Miss Washington," I said. "He's always telling the   33
kids that. We asked Mrs. Wagner, the history teacher, and she said it
means to lie. Like he means I'm a liar."

The look in the principal's eye said, "Oh, you smarty pants bas-   34
tard," but he just smiled and said nothing.

Miss Washington said, "Iffen thar's any pokin' ta be done, we all   35
heah is gonna do it," and she looked hard at the principal. The
crowd looked hard at the principal. Hard sounds were taking
forms, like, "So this is the way they treat our kids in school?" and

"What you-all expect? These heah white people doan give a damn," and "If they evah treats mah boy like that, I'd . . . ."

The principal, smiling softly, began backing up.   36

I heard Momma's voice: "Piri, Piri, *qué pasa?*"   37

"Everything all right, Mis' Thomas," Miss Washington assured   38
her. "This heah man was tryin' to hit your son, but ain't, 'cause I'll break his damn head wide open." Miss Washington shifted her weight forward. "Damn, Ah got a good mind to do it right now," she added.

The principal, remembering the bit about discretion being the   39
better part of valor, split.

Everyone tried to calm Moms down. I felt like everybody there   40
was my family. I let Momma lead me upstairs to our apartment. Everyone patted me on the head as we went by.

"You're going to school with your *padre* in the morning," Momma   41
said.

"Uh-uh, Moms," I said. "That principal will stomp my chest in   42
with that finger of his."

"No he won't, *muchacho*. Your father will go with you an' every-   43
thing will be fixed up."

I just nodded my head and thought how great if would be if Miss   44
Washington could go with me.

A Second Look

1 Thomas uses much direct quotation in his writing. How does he make the voices of Miss Shepard, the principal, and Miss Washington sound different?

2 How is the voice or style of the narrator (the adult Thomas) different from the voice of the student (young Piri)?

3 At the end of paragraph 11, Thomas says, "I hit it." Why does he use the pronoun *it* instead of *her*?

4 What does Thomas mean when he says he smells "a Harlem lynch party in the making" (paragraph 28)? Is he exaggerating?

5 Miss Washington and the principal take sides and act quickly in this situation because they act on the basis of group values that they have accepted. What are these values in each case?

Ideas for Writing

1 Tell about a situation in school or elsewhere in which you found yourself in trouble with those in authority. Begin by setting up the circumstances and introducing the people you will write about. (Notice that Thomas describes Miss Shepard briefly. He doesn't describe the principal at first; we learn about the principal through what he says and does.) Then show how the situation developed, what actions took place, and how it ended.

2 Describe a teacher you liked or disliked very much. You will want to tell what the teacher looked like, how he or she behaved in class, and why you liked or disliked this person. You may use brief stories to help your readers understand what kind of person the teacher was.

3 Look at paragraphs 15 and 16 of Thomas's narrative. His description is alive and exciting because he uses many active, lively verbs. Try writing a paragraph in which you describe some brief but vigorous physical action—for example, running through a crowded place, lifting a heavy weight, passing a football, serving in tennis, chasing or being chased by an animal. Use as many lively and specific verbs as you can.

My First Hunting Trip

John Bennett

Looking Forward

This essay was written by a freshman composition student. As in Langston Hughes's "Salvation," the main idea here concerns the difference between what Bennett expected and what really happened. To make his point, he emphasizes how he feels at different times during the hunting trip.

 Help with Words

foraging *(paragraph 6):* searching for food
replica *(paragraph 6):* a copy
mauling *(paragraph 11):* injuring by rough treatment

It seems as if the cold is what I remember most. 1

The three of us (Tom, Dad, and I) rode in Tom's old pickup, 2 sitting on our hands to keep them warm. I had been on hunting trips before, but this one was different. For the first time, I was allowed to carry a gun—an overused Winchester 20-gauge that was nearly as big as I was.

There was snow on the ground—three, maybe four inches. The 3 drive to our old farm was painfully long, but we arrived just before dawn. We quickly unpacked, loaded our guns, and headed along an old road toward a dense group of briars, fallen trees, and young saplings. The two beagles we had brought along as "flushers" scurried from tree to bush, eagerly sniffing some day-old scent.

When we reached the top of the hill, two rabbits broke behind us. 4
My dad and Tom shot once apiece, missing each time. I mumbled
something about being too cold to move and walked on.

My task, I soon learned, was to sit and wait at the edge of the 5
dense forest while Tom and Dad took the two dogs in. Supposedly,
they would flush the rabbits out so I could get a shot. It sounded a
bit suspicious to me, but I was tired from walking anyway.

I watched them disappear into the brush and sat down on a 6
damp, rotten log. I then concentrated on observing the tree line I
was stationed upon; no movement, not even the slightest change
went unnoticed. After a while, large clumps of grass began to imitate foraging rabbits. Only a sudden gust of wind saved one extremely life-like replica, some forty-five yards away.

I laid my gun on one side of the log and put both my hands inside 7
my wool jacket in a fruitless attempt to keep them warm. It was no
use; my fingers became numb and lifeless. There was no shelter
from the wind, and every five minutes or so I would shake my arms
like an injured bird, trying to create some body heat.

Up ahead, about seventy-five yards, the smaller of the two dogs 8
came out of the foliage, ran toward me for twenty feet, and then was
lost again in the brush. He was obviously on to something.

I suddenly became unaware of the cold as I reached for my gun. 9
The same fingers that just before were blue and numb clicked the
safety off. Trying to get a better look, I stood up above the weeds. I
felt my heart quicken its pace, and I felt myself begin to tremble. Not
from cold, however—I was no longer cold—but I trembled with an
anticipation of what I somehow knew would come. I loosened the
top button of my hunting vest and waited.

The rabbit appeared about fifty yards away, oblivious to my pres- 10
ence. I knew it was too far away for a certain kill shot, so I slowly
knelt down and tried to hide. The rabbit, intent on escaping from
the dog on its trail, came directly toward me until it was in range. I
rose, ready for my prey to bolt away in fear. Instead, the rabbit continued toward me, and then stopped five yards away from the gun
barrel pointed at its head. It sat there, partially obscured by the
snow, mocking the fact that I held its life in my right index finger.

I was confused, uncertain. This wasn't how it was supposed to 11
be, not how I had seen it before. There was no sport (a favorite
hunter's word) in mauling a rabbit sitting fifteen feet away. The
rabbit wouldn't move, even when I stomped my foot in the snow.

I could not let my chance pass. Bracing myself for the recoil of my 12
weapon, I squeezed the trigger and watched my prey fall into the
blood-stained snow.

My trembling had stopped, and I realized that my bottom layer of 13
clothes was soaked with perspiration. I sat down beside the rabbit,
watching its back legs writhe violently.

"Reflexes," I told myself. 14

Tom and Dad approached me from behind. Seeing the rabbit, now 15
still and cold in the snow, they congratulated me on my first kill. I
watched Tom field dress the rabbit as he told me of his first rabbit.

I wasn't listening much. It had become cold again, and I turned 16
my back to the wind.

A Second Look

1 Bennett emphasizes the cold beginning with the first sentence. What
   details indicate how cold he feels? Why does he feel cold again after
   shooting the rabbit?
2 What other kinds of details does the author use in the first three paragraphs?
3 What does paragraph 6 indicate about the author's state of mind? (Note
   that he shows us rather than tells us.)

Ideas for Writing

1 Write a paragraph describing a time when you were unusually cold,
   hot, or wet, for instance. Concentrate on using sense words. To get
   started, list as many words as you can think of that describe how you
   felt. Choose several of the most vivid ones to include in your paragraph.
2 Write about an important experience in your life that taught you something about yourself. Be sure that the main idea is clear, even if it is not
   stated in your essay.

Making Connections

The essays of Langston Hughes, Maxine Hong Kingston, and John Bennett
all recall disillusioning experiences that left the young people with a feeling different from the one their cultures had led them to expect. Is the
disillusionment necessary to their growing up? Does each young person
learn some important reality?

Families

Good Morning, Merry Sunshine

Bob Greene

Looking Forward

On the day Amanda Sue Greene was born, her father, writer Bob Greene, began a journal. For the next year, he kept a promise to himself and his daughter, recording his observations and feelings every day. The following excerpts reflect just a few of the changes that father and daughter experienced during Amanda's first year of life.

 Help with Words

exuberance *(paragraph 1):* enthusiasm, exhilaration
giddiness *(paragraph 1):* flightiness, lightheadedness
pondered *(paragraph 10):* considered, thought about
wary *(paragraph 14):* cautious, distrustful
inhibitions *(paragraph 20):* reserve, checks on emotions or actions
delineate *(paragraph 49):* define, describe
decipher *(paragraph 51):* solve, figure out

June 11

People talk about the emotions that come when a baby is 1 born: exuberance, relief, giddiness, pure ecstasy. The thought that you have seen a miracle in front of your eyes.

I knew I was supposed to be feeling all of those things, and of 2
course I did. But the dominant emotion inside me was a more basic
one. I was scared; scared of what I knew was sure to come, and more
scared about what I didn't know. I am of a generation that has made
self-indulgence a kind of secular religion. I looked down at that
baby, and suddenly I felt that a whole part of my life had just ended,
been cut off, and I was beginning something for which I had no
preparation.

That's what went through me as I watched my baby enter the 3
world; a sense of fear unlike any I have felt in my life. Fear that
sprang from the place where the greatest fears have always lurked:
fear of the totally unknown.

July 11

I went into Amanda's room this morning, and, as I have every 4
morning, I looked down into her crib and said, "Good morning,
merry sunshine." She smiled back.

Today Susan asked me why I was saying it. 5

"I don't know," I said, and I didn't. But I started thinking about it, 6
and I figured it out. "Good morning, merry sunshine" is what my
mother used to say to me every morning when I was a child. I
hadn't heard the words since I was five years old—thirty years ago.
But without being reminded, here I was saying the same thing
every day. I would tell my mother about it, but I think I'm too
embarrassed.

I read in a book somewhere that, before long, a baby figures out 7
that "Dad means fun; mom means work." I think I understand that.
When I pick Amanda up or carry her around, it is to play with her
and to amuse the two of us. When Susan picks her up, it is usually to
feed her or to fix something that is wrong.

Susan has figured that out, too. "What if I hadn't called the doctor 8
yesterday about Amanda's navel?" she said. She knew the truth:
that if the infection had spread, it would have been considered her
fault for not spotting something wrong. That's not how it should be,
but it's how things are. Dad means fun; mom means work.

Susan was sitting on the couch nursing Amanda—who turned 9
one month old today—and I leaned over, took Amanda's hand, and
said, "Do you know that you're going to have to take care of us in
our old age?"

Then I let go of her hand and pondered the fact that it might even   10
be true.

November 20

Sometimes the smallest things almost break my heart.   11

When she is startled, she smiles. There will be a sudden noise   12
from outside; or I will walk into the room unexpectedly; or the
phone will ring.

And she will turn her head toward the direction of the intrusion,   13
and her immediate instinct will be to grin that toothless grin. It is as
if she believes that whatever comes into her world, it is bound to be
pleasant and happy. It does not occur to her that anything might
harm her; every signal she has received so far has told her that
whatever happens will be good.

And of course that will not always be so. The day will come when   14
she learns to be wary; when she learns not to trust anything she
does not know. I think about that when I see her jerk her head and
smile; I make myself pay attention, for soon enough she will have
changed.

I thought it was just me noticing this. But tonight Susan was star-   15
ing at Amanda as she laughed; Susan said, "It's so sad. She's eventually going to have to learn that the world can be awful."

I guess that's right. But for now, we can watch her face light up.   16

March 4

When she was out in public, she used to smile at every stranger who   17
came into view. If there was a new face in her field of vision that face
received a smile.

Now that's stopped.   18

If it's someone she's seen a lot before—clerks in the grocery store,   19
the lady at the cleaners—she will light up and smile as widely as
before. But now if someone new comes up and looks at her and says
something, she will be wary.

It's her inhibitions beginning to develop. Something is telling her   20
that everyone should not automatically be welcomed into her world.

April 3

Tonight Susan put into words what I have been thinking.   21

"I was looking at her sleep," she said, "and I looked down at her   22
. . . and she didn't look like a baby anymore."

"What did she look like?" I said.   23

"Like a little girl," Susan said.   24

And it's true. I've been noticing it, too. She's still a baby, of course,   25
and will be for another year or so. But she's not the kind of baby we
were getting used to. She's not a tiny infant.

She's growing, and her face is taking on its own personality, and   26
her hair is growing thicker; it's butterscotch in color now. It's really
happening; she's beginning to turn into a little girl.

No matter how much attention I pay to her, no matter how hard I   27
try to notice every change in her life, there are certain things that
happen during the moments I'm not watching. I suppose if I watched
twenty-four hours a day, the changes would happen during the
split-seconds when I was blinking. There are certain things so magi-
cal and so mysterious that no one sees them happen. But they happen, all right; you can see them once they've happened. Yes, you
can.

May 17

I had to fly to Grand Rapids, Michigan, for an *Esquire* assignment. I   28
had dinner with some reporters from the local newspaper, then
went back to my hotel room and called Susan.

"She's looking for you," she said.   29

"What do you mean?" I said.   30

"She's crawling around the apartment going 'Da-da,'" Susan   31
said. "She's looking everywhere. I keep telling her that Da-da went
bye-bye, but she thinks you're here somewhere."

That's new. I'm used to the fact that she knows I'm "Da-da," and   32
that she calls out the phrase whenever she sees me. But this is the
first time that she's gone looking for me; before this, it always
seemed that she was conscious of me when I was around, but that
she forgot about me as soon as I left the house.

"She keeps going into your bathroom," Susan said. "She thinks   33
you must be in the shower."

I changed my reservations to get an earlier flight home tomorrow.   34

May 24

She was pushing herself along with that giraffe walker tonight, and   35
every time the walker would come to a stop against a wall, she let
out a scream. She would stop screaming only when we turned the
giraffe around.

"She really is getting spoiled," I said.

"That's not spoiled," Susan said.

"What do you call it?" I said. "From the moment she got the giraffe, she's screamed every time it hits a wall even for a second."

"She just doesn't understand the concept of something stopping," Susan said. "It's completely foreign to her. As far as she's concerned, as long as she pushes the giraffe, it will move forward. She doesn't know how to deal with the idea that something can make it stop."

"What if I screamed every time something didn't go my way?" I said.

"You know," Susan said. "I'm not sure how healthy it is to compare your own emotional development with the emotional development of an eleven-month-old child."

June 10

On the way home from work, I stopped in at a bar I used to frequent in the days before Amanda was born. I felt like a Friday night drink. The bartender—even though we hadn't seen each other much lately—quickly fell into easy conversation with me.

After a while he said, "So what are you going to do this weekend?"

"I'll be at home," I said. "Tomorrow is my daughter's first birthday."

"No!" he said. "It's been a year? I can't believe it. It seems like she was born just the other day. Does it seem like a year to you?"

I just looked across the bar at the mirrored wall. "I don't know," I said.

June 11

It's five o-clock in the morning. I'm in the living room; Amanda and Susan are asleep.

Today my parents and Susan's parents arrive for Amanda's birthday party. Susan has hung crepe paper and balloons; there will be gifts and picture taking.

I don't know why I couldn't sleep; but here I am, looking out the windows and trying to sort out my thoughts. I suppose it's a futile task; maybe some day, years from now, I'll be able to delineate what this year has meant to me. But not now.

All I know is that, here in my home, I have a completely different 50
feeling than I ever expected I'd have. Everything has changed; I
guess I knew that was bound to happen, but I couldn't have pre-
dicted in precisely what ways. Quite simply, I am a different person
than I was a year ago.

I just went into Amanda's room and looked down at her. She 51
never knew me as the man I was before; she may never be aware
that, just by living, she has changed another life so much. Some day
I can try to explain it to her, and she can try to understand; but she
will be attempting to understand the words of a person she knows
only as her father—and it will be too much to expect her to decipher
who that person was before he became her father.

All that can be dealt with later, though. I should be getting back to 52
bed—it's going to be a long day, and it doesn't make sense to start it
exhausted. But something in me doesn't want to sleep; something in
me wants to stay out here alone, in the darkness, and let the un-
focused thoughts drift over me.

So I may still be out here when the sun rises. When I hear the first 53
sound from my daughter's bedroom I will go in and lift her to me,
as I have on so many mornings; as I hope to on so many mornings to
come. There will be one candle on a cake today; I will accept that as
marking the end of this particular story. But the story goes on; it is
unlike any I have ever been a part of, and it goes on.

A Second Look

1 On June 11, in the first entry, Greene writes: "I am of a generation that
has made self-indulgence a kind of secular religion." What does he
mean by this? Why does he feel that with his daughter's birth, "a whole
part of my life had just ended, been cut off"?

2 At the end of the first month (July 11), Greene notes that babies soon
realize "Dad means fun; mom means work." What does this imply?
Does the statement seem to hold in the Greene family?

3 What major change occurs in Amanda between November 20 and
March 4? Why is such a change necessary? Why does her mother consider it "sad"?

4 Sometimes Greene suggests what he does not directly state. What does
he suggest about himself in the entries of May 17, May 24, and June 10?

5 What does Greene mean when he says that the entry of June 11 marks "the end of this particular story. But the story goes on."?

 *Ideas for Writing*

1 If you—as a parent, older sibling, friend, or relative—have observed the first weeks of life for a newborn, describe what the experience was like. Include specific details as well as general impressions. How did the child behave? What effects did the presence of this new life have on other members of the family?

2 If you are not already keeping a journal for this or some other class, try it. Make entries for at least one week. Each day record something that seems important, interesting, instructive, or unusual. These need not be major occurrences, merely things you might later want to recall. (A word of caution: Some people find that keeping a journal can be habit forming!)

Becoming Helpless

Colette Dowling

Looking Forward

This selection from Colette Dowling's book *The Cinderella Complex* explains some of the ways that women are taught dependence and submissiveness within their families at an early age. Dowling's father forcefully argued for her to accept his ideas and attitudes. Her mother was already dominated by the father's stronger personality. Dowling's self-examination leads her to believe that women are often actually afraid to succeed, a problem she calls the Cinderella complex.

 Help with Words

metronome *(paragraph 1):* an instrument for marking time

chronic *(paragraph 1):* long-lasting

elusiveness *(paragraph 2):* the quality of being hard to know or understand

confrontation *(paragraph 2):* a face-to-face conflict

intimidated *(paragraph 2):* made timid

palpable *(paragraph 2):* easily seen

loomed *(paragraph 3):* appeared

didactic *(paragraph 3):* inclined to teach or lecture others

authoritarian *(paragraph 3):* domineering

impinged *(paragraph 3):* crowded in on

lavishing *(paragraph 3):* giving freely

exuded *(paragraph 4):* sent out

disdain *(paragraph 7):* scorn or contempt

digress *(paragraph 7):* to wander from the topic

infusing *(paragraph 7):* pouring into

fledgling *(paragraph 8):* inexperienced or early

ruddy *(paragraph 8):* healthy red

For many years I thought that my problems had to do with my father. Not until I was in my thirties did I begin to suspect that feelings about my mother were part of the inner conflict that had begun developing in me when I was very young. My mother was an even-tempered person, not given to screaming or fits of temper, always there, always waiting when my brother and I came home from school. She took me to dance lessons when I was very small, and later—until I was well into my teens—insisted that I practice the piano every day. She would sit by me and count, as regular and predictable as a metronome. Equally predictable was the afternoon nap she took, the small retreat from the reality of her daily life. She was given to illnesses of a chronic variety: headaches, bursitis, fatigue.

On the surface, there didn't seem to be anything so unusual about her life: she was the typical housewife/mother of her time. And yet . . . that peculiar elusiveness, and the little illnesses, so many of which, I think now (and so does she), were related to unexpressed anger. She avoided confrontation with my father and appeared to us children to be thoroughly intimidated by him. When she did speak out on some issue, the strain it caused her was palpable. She feared him.

In comparison with my mother, my father loomed large and vivid in my life—forceful Father with the big voice, big gestures, rude and sometimes embarrassing ways. He was didactic, authoritarian, and no one who knew him could easily dismiss him. Dislike, yes; there were certainly those who could summon forth that sentiment. But no one could pretend he wasn't there. He forced himself upon the consciousness of those with whom he came into contact; his personality impinged. You thought that he was lavishing attention upon you, but often the conversations seemed to spring more from some hidden need of his own.

I loved him. I adored the sureness he exuded, the idealism, the high, edgy energy. His laboratory in the engineering building at Johns Hopkins University was cool and impressive with its big, cold pieces of equipment. He was The Professor. My mother would refer to him, when speaking with others, as "Dr. Hoppmann." She referred to herself as Mrs. Hoppmann. "Mrs. Hoppmann speaking," she would say, when answering the phone, as if to take refuge of some sort in the formality of the phrase, and in the use of my father's name. We were, in fact, a rather formal family.

In his work—which was his life—my father dealt with chalk, 5 numbers, and steel. In his laboratory were machines. On his desk was a massive paperweight someone in the Metallurgy Department had given him, a hunk of smoothly ground steel with a cold, precisely cut cross at the top. I liked to heft the weight of it in my hand. I also wondered why anyone would ever admire it, as it was neither beautiful nor inspiring.

In the face of my father's demanding personality, my mother 6 seemed to have difficulty holding her own. She was quiet and dutiful, a woman who'd grown up as the fourteenth of sixteen children in a Nebraska farm family. Somewhere along in her sixties, she started—quietly, determinedly—to live her own life, almost in spite of my father. My mother grew tougher and more interesting with age, but when I was growing up she was not tough at all; she was submissive. This same submissiveness was something I saw in virtually every woman I met, growing up—a need to defer to the man who was "taking care of" her, the man on whom she depended for everything.

By the time I entered high school I was bringing my ideas home 7 from school—not to Mother, but to Father. There, at the dinner table, he would dissect them with passionate disdain. Then he would move on, digress, go off on a trip of his own that had little to do with me, but always infusing the conversation with great energy. His energy became my energy, or so I thought.

My father considered it his God-given duty to point me in the 8 direction of truth—specifically, to correct the mistaken attitudes inflicted upon me by the "third-rate intellects" who were my teachers. His own role as teacher was more fascinating to him by far, I think now, than my fledgling development as a learner. At the age of twelve or thirteen I began to pursue what was to become a lifelong ambition: to get my father to shut up. It was a peculiar, mutual dependence that we had: I wanted his attention; he wanted mine. He believed that if I would only sit still and listen, he could hand me the world, whole and flawless, like a peeled pear on a silver plate. I didn't want to sit still, and I didn't want the peeled pear. I wanted to find life on my own, in my own way, to stumble upon it like a surprise in a field—the ruddy if misshapen apple that falls from an unpruned tree.

 *A Second Look*

1 To explain how she gradually lost self-confidence and independence, Dowling describes the differing personalities of her mother and father. Describe in your own words the role model her mother provided.

2 Contrast Dowling's father and mother.

3 When did the conflict between Dowling and her father begin? Describe it.

4 Why, according to Dowling's father, did he force his ideas and attitudes on her? Why did she resent this?

5 A simile is a comparison usually signaled by the words *like* or *as*. In paragraph 8, Dowling uses two similes to explain how her father's attitudes differ from her own. In the first, the world is compared to a "peeled pear on a silver plate." In the second, life is compared to a "ruddy if misshapen apple." Contrast the two attitudes that these similes suggest.

6 In what ways might Dr. Hoppmann's profession have contributed to his personality and behavior?

 *Ideas for Writing*

The title of Dowling's chapter, "Becoming Helpless," suggests that the author's purpose is to analyze the causes that brought about a particular effect, feelings of helplessness and dependency in later life.

Choose an important characteristic of your own personality. Are you shy, fearful, self-confident, studious, religious, and so on? Try to decide what people or places or situations made you the way you are. Make notes as you think about causes and effects in your life. Write down specific details.

You could organize your essay by first describing a particular characteristic. How does it show up in your personality? What difference does it make in your life? Then, in the body of the paper, explain what caused this to be a characteristic of your personality. Describe the cause or causes in detail.

The Great Sisters and Brothers War

Andrew Shanley

Looking Forward

Andrew Shanley explains that conflict among the children in a family, sibling rivalry, is nearly unavoidable. The fighting can be intense and disturbing, but it usually passes with childhood.

 Help with Words

writhing *(paragraph 2):* twisting
ensuing *(paragraph 3):* following
cowering *(paragraph 4):* crouching in fear
impassioned *(paragraph 4):* filled with emotion
glowering *(paragraph 7):* looking with anger
banished *(paragraph 11):* made to go
dastardly *(paragraph 11):* mean
dissuade *(paragraph 13):* persuade not to do something

T he evening had been going especially well. As we often do when entertaining guests with children, we fed the kids first so that the adults could have a quiet dinner. All major events in our lives had just about been covered when our friends' two boys and our two stormed into the dining room, announced that it was time for dessert, then raced into the kitchen. 1

I was clearing the dishes when we heard a crash, followed by a ₂ child's howl. We got to the kitchen in time to see our friends' seven-year-old, Kevin, writhing on the floor and bellowing about killing his brother, Tod, nine.

Physical damage was minimal, but mental anguish was consider- ₃ able. Apparently there had been an argument over who would scoop the ice cream. In the ensuing scuffle, Tod had pushed Kevin to the floor.

Now Tod stood cowering in the corner. His mother was giving ₄ him an impassioned lecture.

"Don't you realize that if you can't get along with your own flesh ₅ and blood you can't get along with anybody?" she was asking. "Don't you understand that nobody in the world loves you more than your brother? And this is how you treat him!"

Tod kept his eyes focused on the floor, no doubt wishing he could ₆ be transported to another planet.

I looked at Kevin, who was wiping tears from his cheeks and ₇ glowering at his brother like a boxer before the bell signaling the start of the next round. His father was leaning over and speaking softly to him.

"I'm sure Tod didn't mean it, Kev," he said. "He just got excited ₈ about the ice cream, that's all. The last thing he'd want to do is hurt you."

I wanted Kevin to answer, "Come off it, Dad; he wanted to knock ₉ my head off and you know it!" I was certain I'd smile and cheer if he did, so I hurried away before his reply.

Did our friends really think that siblings should have total con- ₁₀ trol over their emotions and aggressions? If only Tod's mother had acknowledged how easy it is to fight with a brother or sister, then explained it was up to him, the older brother, to show restraint.

As I wiped the dining room table, I thought about my brother, my ₁₁ sister and I as we were growing up. To call what we experienced sibling rivalry is an understatement; it was more like the Great Brothers and Sisters War. I remembered the time my brother and I locked our sister in the closet and "lost" the key—and the time she hit me with the croquet mallet and fractured my finger. We were all regulars in solitary—our bedrooms—where we were banished in an effort to break our urge to commit such dastardly deeds upon one another.

We were by no means oddballs among our peer group, either. 12 One friend of mine stuck such a big wad of gum in his sister's beloved shoulder-length hair that it had to be clipped back to her ears. I'm sure she got her revenge, too, though I can't recall how. These wars were never-ending.

Siblings know each other's most sensitive buttons as well as 13 when to push them for maximum outrage. Our parents tried every way possible to dissuade us from doing battle, but never told us that fighting with a brother or sister was monstrous and abnormal behavior. Instead, they acknowledged that living together peacefully was difficult, and this was all the more reason to work at it.

"You'd better learn to get along," I can hear my mother telling the 14 three of us as if it were yesterday, "because there will be times when all you'll have is each other."

I think we somehow understood. Even on those days when we 15 were nastiest to one another, when we swore our grudges would last into eternity, we'd still climb into our beds and talk long after the lights were out. In time, the three of us became the best of friends. In fact, my brother and I each stood as best man at the other's wedding.

As parents, we hate to see our children fight. We often feel the 16 blows as if they had landed on us; it hurts to see those we love go against each other. That's natural. But it's important to recognize that problems between sisters and brothers can be part of their competition for our love and attention. And when difficulties do arise, we should make an extra effort to demonstrate our love for them all, possibly focusing it where most needed at that particular moment.

When two young boys are diving for the ice cream, however, it's 17 every man for himself with no regard for bloodlines. Later that evening, Tod was playing with our dog when he fell backward over a coffee table onto the floor. He shouted for help. I watched as Kevin ran over and looked down at his brother wedged between the overturned table and the couch.

"Got yourself in a bit of a fix, big brother, haven't you?" Kevin 18 asked, smiling and enjoying the moment. Then he reached over to offer Tod a hand. "You owe me," he said, as he pulled the older boy to his feet. "I could have gotten you good."

The Great Brothers and Sisters War is often troubling, but as with 19 most wars, it has its own codes, as well as its own cycles. And when the bell sounds for the final round—the one that really counts—our kids usually come out and shake hands.

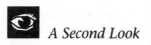 *A Second Look*

1 As many writers do, Shanley captures our attention with an illustration before he states the main idea of his essay. What is his main idea, and in which paragraph do you find it?

2 Shanley's sentences often state his ideas with no wasted words. For these economical sentences to work well, they must be carefully structured. What are the patterns of the second sentence in paragraph 1 and the first sentence in paragraph 3?

3 In paragraph 7, Kevin is compared to a boxer, and in paragraphs 11 and 12 the conflicts between brothers and sisters are described as wars. The essay ends with another reference to boxing. Why does Shanley use this exaggeration?

4 The essay ends by returning to Kevin and Tod. Is the dialogue between the two boys in paragraph 18 true to life? Is this what the boys are likely to have said to each other? Why or why not?

 *Ideas for Writing*

One way to describe the organization of Shanley's essay is to say that it defines the term *sibling rivalry*. The author uses a detailed illustration and several other examples to explain what sibling rivalry is. He also discusses the characteristics of the rivalry and compares it to fighting and war to make it clear.

Choose a term that you understand thoroughly. It might be a term such as *peer pressure*, *generation gap*, *midlife crisis*, or *inferiority complex*. Write an essay in which you try to make the term clear to the reader by giving illustrations of it. What might you compare it to? What does it differ from? Make the term as clear and understandable as possible. Anyone could look up the word in a dictionary, but knowledge from experience will make the term truly understandable. Look at the essays by Marjorie Franco, David Raymond, and Pete Axthelm to see how other writers have developed essays using definition.

Two Dads Are Better Than One?

Angela Waugh

Looking Forward

In this essay written for a freshman composition class, Angela Waugh contrasts her stepfather with her biological father in order to decide which she should care about more. She hopes that looking at their differences will help her decide what her relationship with them should be.

 Help with Words

necessities *(paragraph 1):* basic needs
elders *(paragraph 5):* people who are older
objectively *(paragraph 8):* fairly
obligated *(paragraph 9):* bound by a sense of duty

I 've always envied people with only two parents. They never 1
have to feel sorry for their real father because he is lonely, and
they never have to feel they should care more about their stepfather
because he is the one who has provided them with the necessities
most of their lives.

I, since I have two fathers, have known these feelings. I know 2
what it's like trying to decide which father I should care about more
so that I could tell my friends the next time they asked.

It really should be a clear-cut decision. My two fathers are so ³ different in everything that I should be able to look at these differences and decide.

A major difference between the two is how responsible they are. ⁴ My stepfather has always had a steady job. He enjoys going to work each day and knowing that at the end of the week he'll get a paycheck. With this paycheck he pays bills, buys groceries, and makes sure we all have clothes to wear. On the other hand, my father doesn't particularly care for steady jobs. He is a singer and has worked three or four nights a week in nightclubs most of his life. With his money, he buys things like new guitars and amplifiers. His idea of providing for us, as Mom tells me, is to send ten dollars a month, which is to be divided three ways. He only does this, however, when he's out of state.

Discipline is another major difference between my two fathers. ⁵ My stepfather, who can be very strict at times, believes that children should obey their parents, do what they are told when they are told to do it, and respect their elders. My father, who was never disciplined himself, has quite different views. He has always encouraged my brothers and me to rebel against rules, to ask why we had to do certain things, and to resent being made to do things we thought were stupid. (Going to bed at ten was stupid.) My mother always told us that our father only did this to cause trouble, but I'm not so sure about that. Maybe he did, but then again maybe he thought going to bed at ten was stupid, too!

Education is another big issue my stepfather is concerned about. ⁶ He believes, like many people, that to be able to succeed in life, one has to have a good education. He always told us that he didn't want us to turn out like he did, a truck driver who had to be away from his family for weeks at a time. He used to punish me and my brothers for making C's on our report cards. His theory is that a C is average, and his kids are not average. I wouldn't place any money on that.

My father believes that an education is good to have, but one ⁷ doesn't have to have it to survive. He always says, "Look at me; I made it." I don't think, however, that I would call sleeping in the back of a station wagon "making it"!

So here I have it. All their differences down on paper, and I can ⁸ look at them objectively and decide which father to love more—but it isn't that easy.

I love my father because he is just that, my natural father. I respect 9
him; I am obligated to him, and I want to make him proud of me.
Then there is my stepfather, whom I respect very much; whom I feel
obligated to; whom I want to make proud of me; and, most important of all, whom I have grown to love as much as any child could
possibly love a parent.

I guess I'll never really know which father I love more. I don't see 10
why I should have to love either more. I think I'll just love both of
them in almost equal amounts.

 *A Second Look*

1 Look again at paragraphs 4–7. Write down a word or phrase that states
the main idea of each of these paragraphs. Now check to see what specific information Waugh uses to develop each of these topics.

2 In paragraph 4, what phrase helps Waugh unify her discussion of her
two fathers? Are there words, phrases, or sentences that link ideas in
other paragraphs?

3 Does Waugh's essay suggest an answer to the question asked by the
title?

4 Why do you think Waugh cannot choose between her fathers?

 *Ideas for Writing*

Do you know two people who are somewhat alike but also different? They
might be two friends, two relatives, two teachers, or two roommates. Pick
two such people, and write an essay showing specifically how they are
different.

Begin with one or two paragraphs that introduce your two subjects to the
reader. The body of your paper will focus on the differences. Use at least
one paragraph to develop each major point with facts, examples, or other
supporting details.

Up the Hill

Ryan Hardesty

Looking Forward

Traditions bond families together, bringing present members closer and linking them with the generations that came before them. Not all these traditions are happy ones, but even the sad ones may give families a sense of unity. In this student essay, Ryan Hardesty describes how generations of his Appalachian family have said farewell to their dead.

 Help with Words

treacherous *(paragraph 1):* risky, dangerous
clad *(paragraph 9):* dressed
eerie *(paragraph 9):* strange, ghostly

The black jeep roared into life and began its treacherous jour- 1
ney up the steep, muddy road that led to our family cemetery at the top of the hill. I could see Uncle Jim's bald head near the
back window, and beside him sat my weeping mother, her hands
over her eyes. I couldn't make out any of the other people from this
distance, though I knew they were all relatives, riding up the hill for
my grandmother's funeral. I watched the jeep for several seconds,
until it turned a corner and disappeared behind a clump of pines.

45

"Come on, boy," my grandfather said, placing his broad, weath- 2
ered hand on my shoulder. "Let's go up and say goodbye to your
grandma." I grabbed his hand and we began the long climb to the
cemetery. We had gone only a few yards along the narrow, muddy
road when I began my usual stream of questions.

"Why didn't we ride up, Grandpa?" I asked, staring up into his 3
wrinkled face.

"It didn't seem proper," he answered. He paused for a moment, 4
leaning against an old elm tree. I could tell he was tired because he
was breathing hard. "Ever since I was a little boy, we carried our
people up this mountain. Somehow it don't seem right to take
somebody up in a truck. They ought to be carried, the way 'most
everybody up there was carried, by the people who cared the most.
It seems to me that's the least you can do for a person who's gone."

We started walking again, our feet crunching through the thick 5
covering of dead leaves and sinking into the mud beneath them. It
became steeper here, just above the old elm tree, and I had to struggle to keep moving. I wondered how grandpa could walk so fast as
old as he was. Maybe he was just used to it.

"I've walked this old road many times," Grandpa said, as if he'd 6
read my thoughts, "and it never gets any easier." We paused for a
few minutes. He pulled a ragged yellow handkerchief from his coat
pocket and wiped his forehead. "You know how we used to take people up?" he asked, cramming the handkerchief back into his pocket.

"No," I lied, "how did you take people up?" 7

"We had to carry them, casket and all, clear to the top. It took 8
eight, sometimes ten men to carry somebody up this muletrail, and
it was even worse in those days. We didn't have none of this ridin'
up in trucks and such. We used our own strength to carry our loved
ones home."

He sounded as though he were finished, so I started walking, 9
using the branch I had snapped from the elm as a walking stick. We
were almost at the top now, and I could see the black jeep sitting on
the hillside, its knobby tires deep in the mud. I could see the grandfather oak standing by the gate, guarding the entrance to the cemetery. I could see my darkly clad family standing in a circle, praying
softly. And I could see the shiny black casket sitting on the ground.
Suddenly, everyone began singing, filling the cold air with an eerie,
mournful sound that caused my knees to tremble and my skin to
crawl.

"Did you carry up a lot of people, Grandpa?" I asked, needing 10
the reassurance of my voice to drown out the fear.

"I sure did," he said. He wiped his forehead again, only this time 11
he used the back of his hand. "I helped carry up my papa, right after
I got married. It was a day almost like today, only colder. I remember we slipped in the mud and almost let him slide over the hill. My
two uncles brought Momma up that day, chair and all, because
she was sick and couldn't walk on her own. A few months later I
helped carry up Momma, only this time she didn't need the chair. I
helped carry up your grandma's mother, two uncles, and a few
good friends." His voice sounded funny now, and I realized he was
crying. I walked on ahead and stood beside the grandfather oak,
watching as they lowered grandma into the cold, damp ground.
Everyone was crying, and I think maybe I cried a little too. Then it
was over and time to go home.

As I walked back down, I started thinking about Grandpa. He 12
had carried people up this hill lots of times. It must have hurt as he
watched his friends and family die and be carried up the hill. I wondered if he thought about the day when he would be carried up, and
if he was afraid. Then I thought about myself, a grown man, carrying Momma up the hill like that. And I saw myself . . .

I ran all the way down, my eyes filled with tears and my clothes 13
covered with mud. I caught up with Grandpa, grabbed his hand,
and let him brush away my tears.

I'll hold your hand, Grandpa, I thought, until it's your turn to go. 14
Then, if I'm lucky, somebody will hold my hand until it's my turn.
And I want them to carry me up. None of this riding up in trucks
and such.

 A Second Look

1 Hardesty uses a setting that may not be familiar to many readers. Pick
out some of the details that help us get a clear picture of the location.

2 Writers often use dialogue to suggest (rather than directly state) something about the people they are describing. What does the old man's
speech tell readers about him? Does his speech sound realistic?

3 What is the grandfather's attitude about transporting the dead to the cemetery? Why does he feel this way?

4 What details in the essay indicate that this family tradition will be carried on by the next generation?

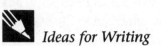 *Ideas for Writing*

Write about a tradition in your own family. Besides burial customs, there are many traditions: celebrating holidays, observing birthdays, holding weddings, going to reunions, and so forth. You might describe how such a tradition is carried out over time—for example, telling your readers how your family celebrates Christmas year after year or how they gather annually for grandfather's birthday. On the other hand, you might focus on one particular occasion—a particular Thanksgiving dinner, a specific Seder, the 1990 family reunion held on the Fourth of July, your sixteenth birthday party—that will provide a concrete example of how the tradition is observed.

Making Connections

The essays of Bob Greene, Colette Dowling, and Angela Waugh all provide descriptions of the relationships of four fathers with their daughters. How are these fathers different in their actions and attitudes? Can you find any similarities among them?

Laughter

After a Fall

Garrison Keillor

Looking Forward

Laughing at a fall in which no one is hurt is a typical reaction. Garrison Keillor, a writer and comedian, admits that laughing is a natural response, but he then goes on to examine the feelings of the person who has fallen. The victim is likely to view the fall differently. Notice the carefully chosen words that help the reader see the actions Keillor describes.

 ### Help with Words

adrenaline *(paragraph 1):* a hormone produced especially in frightening situations

prone *(paragraph 1):* inclined, likely to experience

inexplicable *(paragraph 1):* not explainable

smirk *(paragraph 3):* a knowing smile

rigorous *(paragraph 3):* demanding

artifacts *(paragraph 3):* man-made objects or tools

perspective *(paragraph 4):* a way of looking at a subject

fundamentalist *(paragraph 14):* holding religious beliefs based on a literal interpretation of the Bible

constricted *(paragraph 14):* limited

inevitable *(paragraph 14):* unavoidable

nonchalant *(paragraph 15):* unconcerned

venture *(paragraph 18):* undertaking, experience

W hen you happen to step off an edge you didn't see and   1
lurch forward into space waving your arms, it's the end
of the world for a second or two, and after you do land, even if you
know you're O.K. and no bones are broken it may take a few seconds to decide whether this is funny or not. Your body is still
worked up about the fall—especially the nervous system and the
adrenaline-producing areas. In fact, I am still a little shaky from a
spill that occurred two hours ago, when I put on a jacket, walked
out the front door of this house here in St. Paul, Minnesota, and for
no reason whatever took a plunge down five steps and landed on
the sidewalk flat on my back with my legs up in the air. I am thirty-
nine years old and in fairly good shape, not prone to blackouts or
sudden dizziness, and so a sudden inexplicable fall comes as a big
surprise to me.

A woman who was jogging down the street—a short, muscular   2
young woman in a gray sweatshirt and sweatpants—stopped and
asked if I was O.K. "Yeah! Fine!" I said and got right up. "I just fell, I
guess," I said. "Thanks," I said. She smiled and trotted away.

Her smile has followed me into the house, and I see it now as a   3
smirk, which is what it was. She was too polite to bend over and
hoot and shriek and guffaw and cackle and cough and whoop and
wheeze and slap her thighs and stomp on the ground, but it was
there in that smile: a young woman who through rigorous physical
training and feminist thinking has gradually been taking charge of
her own life and ridding her attic of self-hatred and doubt and fear
and mindless competitiveness and other artifacts of male-domi-
nated culture is rewarded with the sight of a middle-aged man in a
brown suit with a striped tie falling down some steps as if someone
had kicked him in the pants.

I'm sorry if I don't consider this humorous. I would like to. I wish   4
she had come over and helped me up and then perhaps sat on the
steps with me while I calmed down. We might have got to talking
about the fall and how each of us viewed it from a different perspective. . . .

I might have seen it her way, but she ran down the street, and   5
now I can only see my side of the fall. I feel old and achy and ridiculous and cheapened by the whole experience. I understand now

why my son was so angry with me a few months ago when he tripped on a shoelace and fell in the neighbor's yard—a yard where the neighbor's sheepdog had lived for years—and I cackled at him.

"It's not funny!" he yelled.   6

"Oh, don't be so sensitive," I said.   7

Don't be so sensitive! What a dumb thing to say! Who has the   8
right to tell someone else how to feel? It is the right of the person who falls in the dog droppings to decide for himself or herself how he or she will feel. It's not up to a jury. The fallen person determines whether it's funny or not. . . .

Five years ago, I got on a bus with five musicians and rode   9
around for two weeks doing shows every night. They played music; I told jokes and sang a song. One night, in the cafeteria of a junior college in southern Minnesota, we happened to draw a big crowd, and the stage—four big plywood sheets on three-foot steel legs— was moved back twenty feet to make room for more chairs. The show was late starting, the room was stuffy, the crowd was impatient, and when finally the lights dimmed and the spotlight shone on the plywood, I broke from the back door and made a run for the stage, thinking to make a dramatic entrance and give these fine people the show they were waiting for.

What I could not see in the dark was the ceiling and a low con-   10
crete overhang that the stage had been moved partly under, and then the spotlight caught me straight in the eyes and I couldn't see anything. I leaped up onto the stage, and in mid-leap my head hit concrete and my right leg caught the plywood at mid-shin. I toppled forward, stuck out my hands, and landed on my hands and knees. The crowd drew a long breath. I got right up—I had been doing shows long enough to know not to lie onstage and cry in front of a paying audience—and, seeing the microphone about ten feet ahead, strode up to it and held out my arms and said, "Hello everybody! I'm happy to be here!"

Then they laughed—a big thunderstorm of a laugh and a big   11
round of applause for what they now saw had been a wonderful trick. But it wasn't funny! My neck hurt! I hurt all over! On the other hand, to see a tall man in a white suit jump directly into a ceiling and then fall down—how often does a person get to see that? Men dive off high towers through fiery hoops into tiny tanks, men rev up motorcycles and leap long rows of trucks and buses, but I am the only man in show business who takes a good run and jumps

Straight Up Into Solid Concrete Using Only His Bare Head. Amazing! . . .

Oh, it is a sad story, except for the fact that it isn't. My ceiling 12 jump got the show off to a great start. The band played three fast tunes, and I jumped carefully back onstage and did a monologue that the audience, which now knew I was funny, laughed at a lot. Even I, who had a headache, thought it was funny. I really did feel lucky.

So do I still—a tall man who fell now sitting down to write his 13 memoirs. The body is so delicate, the skeleton so skinny; we are stick men pencilled in lightly, with a wooden stick cage to protect the heart and lungs and a cap of bone over the brain. I wonder that I have survived so many plunges, so many quick drops down the short arc that leads to the ground. . . .

The first time I ever went naked in mixed company was at the 14 house of a girl whose father had a bad back and had built himself a sauna in the corner of the basement. Donna and I were friends in college. Both of us had grown up in fundamentalist Christian homes, and we liked to compare notes on that. We both felt constricted by our upbringings and were intent on liberating ourselves and becoming more free and open and natural. So it seemed natural and inevitable one night to wind up at her house with some of her friends there and her parents gone and to take off our clothes and have a sauna.

We were nineteen years old and were very cool ("Take off my 15 clothes? Well, sure. Heck, I've taken them off dozens of times") and were careful to keep cool and be nonchalant and not look at anybody below the neck. We got into the sauna as if getting on the bus. People do this, I thought to myself. There is nothing unusual about it! Nothing! We all have bodies! There is no reason to get excited! This is a normal part of life!

We filed into the little wooden room, all six of us, avoiding unnec- 16 essary body contact, and Donna poured a bucket of water on the hot rocks to make steam. It was very quiet. "There's a shower there on the wall if you want to take a shower," she said in a strange, nervous voice.

"Hey! How about a shower!" a guy said in a cool-guy voice, and 17 he turned on the water full blast. The shower head leaped from the wall. It was a hand-held type—a nozzle at the end of a hose—and it jumped out at us like a snake and thrashed around exploding ice-cold water. He fell back, someone screamed, I slipped and fell, Donna fell on top of me, we leaped apart, and meanwhile the nozzle danced and flew from the force of the blast of water. Donna ran out of the sauna and slipped and fell on the laundry-room floor, and another girl yelled, "God damn you, Tom!" Donna scrambled to her feet. "God! Oh, God!" she cried. Tom yelled, "I'm sorry!" Another guy laughed a loud, wicked laugh, and I tiptoed out as fast as I could move, grabbed my clothes, and got dressed. Donna grabbed her clothes. "Are you all right?" I said, not looking at her or anything. "No!" she said. Somebody laughed a warm, appreciative laugh from inside the sauna. "Don't laugh!" she yelled. "It isn't funny! It isn't the least bit funny!"

"I'm not laughing," I said, though it wasn't me she was angry at. I 18 still am not laughing. I think it's a very serious matter, twenty years later. Your first venture as a naked person, you want it to go right and be a good experience, and then some joker has to go pull a fast one. . . .

I haven't seen you since that night, Donna. I've told the sauna 19 story to dozens of people over the years, and they all thought it was funny but I still don't know what you think. Are you all right?

 *A Second Look*

1 Keillor opens the essay with a personal experience. In what paragraph does he state the main idea of the essay? What is it?

2 What does Keillor mean when he says in paragraph 3 that the woman's smile "followed me into the house"?

3 In paragraph 3, Keillor chooses unusual verbs to describe the way he imagines the woman would like to laugh at him. Explain why the description is amusing.

4 Look carefully at the way Keillor tells about his experience in the sauna. Describe some of the techniques that make the story amusing.

5 Why does Keillor end the essay with a question addressed to Donna? Why does he ask this particular question?

Ideas for Writing

1 Most people could add to Garrison Keillor's essay examples of funny or embarrassing falls they have had. In a paragraph or two, tell about some spill you have taken. Explain how it happened and what you looked like. Work especially on using detailed description that will help the reader imagine the actions. The test for success in this paper is whether the reader can see what you describe.

2 Victims of falls are like victims of jokes: They are expected to laugh at themselves and think no more about it. Have you ever been the butt of a joke that was funny to everyone except you? Write an essay in which you describe the joke and then explain your reaction to it. Try to make the reader understand your side of the story.

Chicken Gizzards

James A. Perkins

Looking Forward

"Chicken Gizzards" is about a humorous experience remembered from childhood. In this sketch, James Perkins—a teacher and the author of short stories, poems, and radio and TV scripts—makes a point about the joy of competition as well as the joy of eating gizzards.

 Help with Words

flanked *(paragraph 1):* placed at the sides
din *(paragraph 4):* a loud noise
strategy *(paragraph 5):* a plan for achieving a specific result
visions *(paragraph 5):* persons or events seen only in the mind
spiel *(paragraph 5):* a sales pitch
groused *(paragraph 7):* complained

D addy and his daddy, Pap, and daddy's brother-in-law, Uncle Eddie, all loved to eat. Whenever our family got together it was around a table, a table loaded with food. I always hoped for ham, but their favorite was fried chicken, and there was usually a heaping platter of fried chicken flanked by steaming bowls of green beans and mashed potatoes and gravy. 1

Besides liking chicken, they all three liked the gizzard best of all, and down underneath of those wings and drumsticks and thighs 2 and whatnot was the one gizzard. I think it all started one Sunday when Pap picked up the platter, smiled sheepishly and said, "Would any of y'all like this here chicken craw?" "Don't mind if I do," said Daddy, and he forked the gizzard right off the platter. Pap's eyes went hard. He just sat there holding that empty platter with both hands. Finally he set it down and said, "I see." From then on we all saw that it was war, and it lasted for years.

At first it was rather crude. Daddy took a wing and passed the chicken to Uncle Eddie. He slid the back off the platter and casually swept the gizzard with it. I could tell by the way they looked at him when he set the empty platter down that he had broken the rules and the last easy victory had been won. 3

Piece by piece another Sunday's chicken was eaten, and the three of them finally sat there staring at the gizzard. When Pap's wife, Lucy, asked, "One of you going to eat that thing?" she was ignored. Finally Pap made his move. There was an awful din of clashing metal and screaming. Pap forked the gizzard. Daddy, like an old time sheriff letting the hired gun slap leather first, nailed that gizzard to the platter with a fork, and Uncle Eddie, who, being right-handed, was at a disadvantage having to reach across, stuck his fork in the back of Pap's hand. 4

It was about then that strategy was introduced. "My Gawd. It looks like Fronk's barn's on fire," yelled Pap. Daddy and Uncle Eddie didn't see any fire out the window. When they turned back they didn't see any gizzard either, and Pap was laughing so hard he nearly choked on it. After that there were so many visions that you would have thought we were a family of Roman Catholics instead of dyed-in-the-wool, dull-as-paint Presbyterians. Pap saw things out the window. Daddy saw things out the back door. Uncle Eddie, who sat facing the china cupboard, was again at somewhat of a disadvantage. One time he told about the woman selling Bibles door to door, whose panties fell off right in the middle of the sales spiel, and gobbled the gizzard whole while Pap and Daddy were laughing. Another time he just sat there staring up at the ceiling. That didn't work. Pap said, "You can't treat us like a bunch of green horns at the county fair. That ceiling's been up there since the house was built, and I ain't taking my eyes off that gizzard." 5

Toward the end nobody believed anybody or anything. One Sunday afternoon the fire bell rang and the three of them just sat there 6 staring at the gizzard, each of them convinced that one of the other two had paid Curly Beckett to ring the bell.

It all came to an end on a Thanksgiving. They hunted all morning and came in to a big chicken dinner. When all the wings and legs and whatnot were gone, there on the platter were three gizzards. "Mr. Macklin gave them to me extra when I bought the chicken," said Lucy. They ignored her. They just sat there sullenly looking at those three gizzards. Pap finally forked one of them and groused, "Who the Hell ever heard of a chicken havin' three gizzards?"

 *A Second Look*

1 Words that appeal to the five senses make writing more lively. Which of the senses are appealed to by the description in paragraph 1? Look at other paragraphs to find words that appeal to the senses.

2 Daddy, Pap, and Uncle Eddie have various tricks for getting the gizzard. List them in the order in which they occur in the sketch. Why does the author use this order?

3 Lucy tries to be helpful by cooking three gizzards for Thanksgiving, but her help is not appreciated. What does she fail to understand?

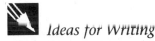 *Ideas for Writing*

1 List a dozen or so sights that are pleasant to you. Look over the list to see whether there is a pattern. Try to draw a generalization about sights that please you. (For example, "I enjoy looking at scenes that remind me of fall in my home town," or "I like to see things around me that make my room cozy and comfortable," or "I like to look at strange and unfamiliar places.") Then go through the same process for the other senses: hearing, smell, taste, and touch. In each case, make a generalization from the list.

For the writing assignment, write three paragraphs using three of the generalizations as topic sentences. Develop the paragraphs by using details from the lists. Each paragraph should be about fifty words long. Note that these are three separate paragraphs; they should not be related to each other.

2 Describe for a group of classmates a humorous incident that occurred at a family gathering. Begin by jotting down all the details you remember about the incident. Next, select only those details that will help your readers understand what made this occurrence funny to you. When you begin writing the description, be sure the introduction makes clear when the incident happened and who was involved.

Pranks for the Memory

Dave Barry

Looking Forward

In his regular columns for the *Miami Herald*, humorist Dave Barry likes to look at the slightly (or sometimes very) ridiculous side of life. In this essay, Barry describes some amusing—and most "unscary"—traditions associated with Halloween. Some are new to the 1990s; others go back at least as far as Barry's boyhood.

 Help with Words

confronted *(paragraph 4):* faced

inedible *(paragraph 8):* not eatable

Druid *(paragraph 10):* member of a Celtic order of priests, soothsayers, judges, and others in pre-Christian Britain, Ireland, and France

Stonehenge *(paragraph 10):* an ancient British structure built of huge free-standing stones (some weighing 30 tons), at one time associated with the Druids

I love Halloween. And not just because it gives us a chance to buy a new mailbox. No, what I love most is the fun of opening our front door and hearing a group of costumed youngsters happily shout out the traditional Halloween greeting: "(Nothing)."

At least that's what traditionally happens at our house. The 2
youngsters just stand there, silent. They have no idea that I have
opened the door. They are as blind as bats, because their eyes are
not lined up with the eyeholes in their costume masks.

Poorly aligned eyeholes are an ancient Halloween tradition, dat- 3
ing back at least as far as my childhood in Armonk, New York. My
early Halloween memories consist of staggering around disguised
as a ghost, unable to see anything except the bed sheet and conse-
quently bonking into trees, falling into brooks, etc. The highlight of
my ghost career came in the 1954 Halloween parade, when I
marched directly into the butt of a horse.

Today's children, of course, do not wear bed sheets. They wear 4
manufactured costumes representing licensed Saturday-morning
cartoon characters and purchased from the Toys "Я" A Billion-Dol-
lar Industry store, but I am pleased to note that the eyeholes still
don't line up. So when I open the door on Halloween, I am confronted with three or four imaginary heroes such as G.I. Joe, Conan
the Barbarian, Oliver North, etc., all of whom would look very terrifying except that they are three feet tall and facing in random direc-
tions. They stand there silently for several seconds, then an adult
voice hisses from the darkness behind them: *"Say 'Trick or Treat,'
dammit!"*

This voice of course belongs to good old Dad, who wants more 5
than anything to be home watching the World Series and eating taco
dip in bulk, but who must instead accompany the children on their
trick-or-treat rounds to make sure I don't put razor blades in the
candy. This is a traditional Halloween danger that the local perky
TV news personalities warn us about every year, using the Frowny
Face they put on when they have to tell us about Bad News, such as
plane crashes and rainy weekends.

So I understand why good old Dad has to be there, but he makes 6
me nervous. I can feel him watching me suspiciously from somewhere out there, and I think to myself: What if he's armed? There is
a reasonable concern, because I live in South Florida, where *nuns*
are armed. So I am very careful about the way I hand out treats.

"Well, boys or perhaps girls!" I say to the licensed characters, in a 7
voice so nonthreatening as to make Mr. Rogers sound like Darth
Vader. "How about some NICE CANDY in its ORIGINAL PACKAGING
that you can clearly see when I hold it up to the porch light here has
NOT BEEN TAMPERED WITH?" Alerted by the sound of my voice, the

licensed characters start lurching blindly toward me, thrusting out trick-or-treat bags already containing enough chocolate to meet the nation's zit needs well into the next century.

Of course there is more to Halloween than massive carbohydrate 8 overdoses. There is also the tradition of bitching about pumpkin prices, a tradition that my wife and I enjoy engaging in each year after paying as much as $20 for a dense inedible fruit so that some pumpkin rancher can put a new Jacuzzi in his Lear jet. This is followed by the tradition of scooping the insides, or technically, the "goop," out of the pumpkin, a chore that always falls to me because both my wife and son refuse to do it, and not without reason, what with the alarming increase in pumpkin-transmitted diseases. (Get the facts! Call the American Pumpkin Council! Don't mention my name!)

But I consider the risk of permanent disfigurement to be a small 9 price to pay for the excitement that comes when I finally finish carving Mr. Jack O'Lantern and put him out on the front porch, there to provide hours of pleasure for the trick-or-treating youngsters except that (a) they can't see and (b) Mr. Jack O'Lantern immediately gets his face kicked into mush by older youngsters playing pranks.

Pranks—defined as "activities that struck you as truly hilarious 10 when you were a teenager but, now that you are a property owner, make you wish you had a high-voltage fence"—are another ancient Halloween tradition. The first Halloween prank ever, played by a group of Druid teenagers, was Stonehenge ("HEY! You kids GET THOSE ROCKS OFF MY LAWN!!"). I can't really complain about the pranks, because as a youth I played several thousand myself. In fact, I figure there must be a God of Prank Justice, who keeps track of everything we do when we're young and then uses Halloween to settle the score ("OK, that's his 14th mailbox. He has 57 to go."). Vastly enjoying this spectacle, I bet, are the ghosts of all my former victims. Assuming they can see through their eyeholes.

 A Second Look

1 Barry appeals to readers by mentioning several aspects of Halloween that are familiar to everyone who has celebrated that night. What are some of them?

2 How has Halloween changed since Barry was a boy? How has it remained the same?

3 Writers are often told they should rarely (if ever) begin a sentence with a coordinating conjunction (for example, *and, but, so*); however, Barry does this frequently. He also ends his essay with a sentence fragment. Why does he deliberately break these "rules" of writing?

4 This essay is loosely organized, but it is not *un*organized. Look at the beginnings of paragraphs to see how Barry makes transitions from one point to another.

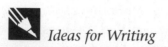 *Ideas for Writing*

Choose an aspect of Halloween (or some other holiday) that you find amusing, and describe it from your personal point of view. If you choose a holiday with which some of your readers may be unfamiliar, briefly explain its significance and a few of its traditions.

This type of essay is fun to write and to read, but remember that informal writing is not disorganized writing. Be sure that your reader can follow your ideas clearly from paragraph to paragraph.

The First Kiss

Steven Graves

Looking Forward

In this freshman essay, a student remembers an important event in his life. Notice that the amused attitude is that of the mature Steven Graves looking back, not that of young Stevie Graves, the first-grader being described.

Help with Words

burr-headed *(paragraph 1):* having a short haircut
incredible *(paragraph 1):* unbelievable
virile *(paragraph 2):* manly
knickers *(paragraph 4):* knee-length pants

O f parades and circus trips and all those anxiously awaited jaunts to Grandmother's or the ice cream parlor, the most memorable occasion of all was my first kiss. The electricity that went through my body and soul was enough to light Manhattan. Every hair on my burr-headed little body stood on end. The nights afterward weren't long enough to handle the incredible dreams that rushed through my head.

There I was, Stevie Graves, "Peaches" to my friends, young and virile, finely tuned body, masculine approach to problems, and sporting one of the most beautiful flattops in the first grade at Ewing Elementary School. My uncle, who was older, a fourth grader, had explained the process of the first kiss to me, and I was ready. He went on to explain more, but I decided I would perfect one thing at a time.

Now I'm not saying I didn't already have a grasp of kissing. My 3
mother and dad never kissed when I could see them, but my cousin
Jane was all lips. She and her boyfriend used to kiss for hours and
hours, even days. I thought they were going to die from lack of air
once. I couldn't see much except lips through that keyhole, but that
was enough to cause strange feelings in me.

I had been in love with a girl named Debbie ever since I started 4
kindergarten, and I knew that when the moment was just right, she
was going to be the one. And she was. There I stood, grammar book
in one hand, a copy of *Daisy the Cow* in the other, and my knickers
bound tight around my knees. No, that's a lie. I never had knickers,
but my stance on the front steps of the school that day must have
looked very noble anyway.

We had been writing to each other for months about getting to- 5
gether for a kiss or two, but now it was going to happen. Here she
came off the bus, bouncing like a basketball, hair in braids, teeth in
braces, just bursting with youth and excitement, ready for—yes, the
kiss. She ran towards me, and I knew it was now. She passed me by,
but then she turned, ran back, and planted the most beautiful kiss
on my cheek. I was electric, caught at the top of the ferris wheel of
first-grade sexual response.

As years passed, I forgot about Debbie, but that kiss will always 6
be a place, a time, an experience I'll never forget. If only I could be
there again, waiting anxiously to be swept off my feet by a gentle
peck on the cheek.

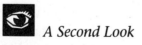 *A Second Look*

1 How does the author create humor in this essay?
2 The essay is not as loosely organized as it first appears to be. Briefly
   outline the organization.
3 Pick out several descriptive words or phrases, and explain why you
   consider them to be effective. Pay particular attention to paragraph 5.

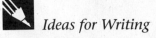

Ideas for Writing

1 Tell about an emotion-filled experience from your elementary-school days. This kind of paper needs careful organization. Begin by indicating the subject (such as a first kiss) and setting up the situation. Then tell about the event itself. Be sure the action is described in the order in which it occurred. If you wish, you may close by looking back from the present and commenting on this emotional experience.

2 In a paragraph, describe yourself as a first grader. Include details about your appearance and your feelings. Your description may be completely factual, or like Steven Graves's self-portrait, it may include slight humorous exaggeration.

Making Connections

Reconsider the essays in this unit to decide which of them use humor to make a serious point. Decide what point is made in each case. Why is humor sometimes an effective way to communicate serious ideas?

Differences

Halfway to Dick and Jane

Jack Agueros

Looking Forward

The son of Puerto Rican immigrants, Jack Agueros grew up in Spanish Harlem. The differences he writes about are caused by both passing time and varying ethnic backgrounds.

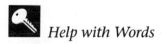 *Help with Words*

dismantle *(paragraph 2):* take apart

plantain *(paragraph 2):* a large plant with leaves and fruit similar to the banana

compensation *(paragraph 2):* payment

foyer *(paragraph 2):* entrance hall

declaim *(paragraph 2):* recite dramatically

immaculate *(paragraph 3):* spotlessly clean

railroad flat *(paragraph 5):* a narrow apartment with the rooms connecting in a single line and with doors front and back

intensified *(paragraph 7):* made stronger

pathetically *(paragraph 7):* very sadly

pathologically *(paragraph 7):* in an unhealthy or diseased way

I am an only child. My parents and I always talked about my becoming a doctor. The law and politics were not highly regarded in my house. Lawyers, my mother would explain, had to defend people whether they were guilty or not, while politicians, my father would say, were all crooks. A doctor helped everybody, rich and poor, white and black. If I became a doctor, I could study hay fever and find a cure for it, my godmother would say. Also, I could take care of my parents when they were old. I liked the idea of helping, and for nineteen years my sole ambition was to study medicine.

My house had books, not many, but my parents encouraged me   2 to read. As I became a good reader they bought books for me and never refused me money for their purchase. My father once built a bookcase for me. It was an important moment, for I had always believed that my father was not too happy about my being a book-worm. The atmosphere at home was always warm. We seemed to be a popular family. We entertained frequently, with two standing parties a year—at Christmas and for my birthday. Parties were al-ways large. My father would dismantle the beds and move all the furniture so that the full two rooms could be used for dancing. My mother would cook up a storm, particularly at Christmas. *Pasteles, lechon asado, arroz con gandules,* and a lot of *coquito* to drink (meat-stuffed plantain, roast pork, rice with pigeon peas, and coconut nog). My father always brought in a band. They played without compensation and were guests at the party. They ate and drank and danced while a victrola covered the intermissions. One year my father brought home a whole pig and hung it in the foyer doorway. He and my mother prepared it by rubbing it down with oil, oreg-ano, and garlic. After preparation, the pig was taken down and car-ried over to a local bakery where it was cooked and returned home. Parties always went on till daybreak, and in addition to the band, there were always volunteers to sing and declaim poetry.

My mother kept an immaculate household. Bedspreads (chenille   3 seemed to be very in) and lace curtains, washed at home like every-thing else, were hung up on huge racks with rows of tight nails. The racks were assembled in the living room, and the moisture from the wet bedspreads would fill the apartment. In a sense, that seems to be the lasting image of that period of my life. The house was clean. The neighbors were clean. The streets, with few cars, were clean. The buildings were clean and uncluttered with people on the stoops. The park was clean. The visitors to my house were clean, and the relationships that my family had with other Puerto Rican families, and the Italian families that my father had met through baseball and my mother through the garment center, were clean. Second Avenue was clean and most of the apartment windows had awnings. There was always music, there seemed to be no rain, and snow did not become slush. School was fun, we wrote essays about how grand America was, we put up hunchbacked cats at Halloween, we believed Santa Claus visited everyone. I believed everyone was Catholic. I grew up with dogs, nightingales, my godmother's guitar, rocking chair, cat, guppies, my father's occasional roosters, kept in a cage on the fire escape. Laundry delivered and collected by horse and wagon, fruits and vegetables sold the same way, windowsill refrigeration in winter, iceman and box in summer. The police my friends, likewise the teachers.

In short, the first seven or so years of my life were not too great a 4 variation on Dick and Jane, the school book figures who, if my memory serves me correctly, were blond Anglo-Saxons, not immigrants, not migrants like the Puerto Ricans, and not the children of either immigrants or migrants.

My family moved in 1941 to Lexington Avenue into a larger 5 apartment where I could have my own room. It was a light, sunny, railroad flat on the top floor of a well-kept building. I transferred to a new school, and whereas before my classmates had been mostly black, the new school had few blacks. The classes were made up of Italians, Irish, Jews, and a sprinkling of Puerto Ricans. My block was populated by Jews, Italians, and Puerto Ricans.

And then a whole series of different events began. I went to junior 6 high school. We played in the backyards, where we tore down fences to build fires to cook stolen potatoes. We tore up whole hedges, because the green tender limbs would not burn when they were peeled, and thus made perfect skewers for our stolen "mickies." We played tag in the abandoned buildings, tearing the plaster off the walls, tearing the wire lath off the wooden slats, tearing the wooden slats themselves, good for fires, for kites, for sword fighting. We ran up and down the fire escapes playing tag and over and across many rooftops. The war ended and the heavy Puerto Rican migration began. The Irish and the Jews disappeared from the neighborhood. The Italians tried to consolidate east of Third Avenue.

What caused the clean and open world to end? Many things. Into 7 an ancient neighborhood came pouring four to five times more people than it had been designed to hold. Men who came running at the promise of jobs were jobless as the war ended. They were confused. They could not see the economic forces that ruled their lives as they drank beer on the corners, reassuring themselves of good times to come while they were hell-bent toward alcoholism. The sudden surge in numbers caused new resentments, and prejudice was intensified. Some were forced to live in cellars, and were then characterized as cave dwellers. Kids came who were confused by the new surroundings; their Puerto Ricanness forced us against a mirror asking, "If they are Puerto Ricans, what are we?" and thus they confused us. In our confusion we were sometimes pathetically reaching out, sometimes pathologically striking out. Gangs. Drugs. Wine. Smoking. Girls. Dances and slow-drag music. Mambo. Spics, Spooks, and Wops. Territories, brother gangs, and war councils establishing rules for right of way on blocks and avenues and for seating in the local theater. Pegged pants and zip guns. Slang.

Dick and Jane were dead, man. Education collapsed. Every class-   8
room had ten kids who spoke no English. Black, Italian, Puerto Rican relations in the classroom were good, but we all knew we couldn't visit one another's neighborhoods. Sometimes we could not move too freely within our own blocks. On 109th, from the lamp post west, the Latin Aces, and from the lamp post east, the Senecas, the "club" I belonged to. The kids who spoke no English became known as Marine Tigers, picked up from a popular Spanish song. (The Marine Tiger and the Marine Shark were two ships that sailed from San Juan to New York and brought over many, many migrants from the island.)

The neighborhood had its boundaries. Third Avenue and east,   9
Italian. Fifth Avenue and west, black. South, there was a hill on 103rd Street known locally as Cooney's Hill. When you got to the top of the hill, something strange happened: America began, because from the hill south was where the "Americans" lived. Dick and Jane were not dead: they were alive and well in a better neighborhood.

When, as a group of Puerto Rican kids, we decided to go swim-   10
ming to Jefferson Park Pool, we knew we risked a fight and a beating from the Italians. And when we went to La Milagrosa Church in Harlem, we knew we risked a fight and a beating from the blacks. But when we went over Cooney's Hill, we risked dirty looks, disapproving looks, and questions from the police like, "What are you

doing in this neighborhood?" and "Why don't you kids go back where you belong?"

Where we belonged! Man, I had written compositions about America. Didn't I belong on the Central Park tennis courts, even if I didn't know how to play? Couldn't I watch Dick play? Weren't these policemen working for me too? . . .

 A Second Look

1 Dick and Jane were the white, middle-class characters in a series of reading textbooks once very popular in lower elementary school. What does Agueros mean by "Halfway to Dick and Jane"? What does he mean when he refers to the characters again in paragraphs 8, 9, and 11?

2 What differences occur after Agueros moves to Lexington Avenue? What are the causes of these differences?

3 In paragraph 7, Agueros says that when new immigrant kids moved into the neighborhood, "their Puerto Ricanness forced us against a mirror asking, 'If they are Puerto Ricans, what are we?'" What does he mean by this?

4 Beginning in paragraph 7, there are some changes in the author's style, especially in his word choice and sentence structure. What are these changes, and why do you think he makes them?

5 If you have read the selection from Maxine Hong Kingston's *The Woman Warrior*, compare her experience with that of Jack Agueros. How were their childhoods similar, and how were they different? Do you think Kingston, as she is described in this selection, would describe herself as "halfway to Dick and Jane"? Explain why or why not.

 *Ideas for Writing*

1 If you are the child of immigrant parents (or perhaps if you know well someone else who is), then you too may understand what it is like to be caught between two cultures. If so, describe this feeling.

Explain how it feels to move away from one culture and toward another. You might consider such questions as these: Do you feel good or bad about this experience? Are you moving voluntarily from one culture to another, or do you feel you are being forced? Do you resent either cultural group or perhaps both? What are the advantages and disadvantages of the move? Use specific details and brief descriptions of specific experiences to show your readers how you feel. Assume that your readers are of various ethnic or cultural backgrounds; that is, they are not all Hispanic, all black, all white, and so on.

2   A policeman says to Agueros and his friends: "Why don't you kids go back where you belong?" Has anyone ever made you feel as if you didn't belong? If so, describe that experience. Tell your readers what the situation was, who said you did not belong, and how you reacted to that charge.

3   Have you ever lived in a neighborhood or a community that went through a major change, growing either better or worse? If so, write about the experience. Explain to your readers (who may not be familiar with the place you are describing) how the place was before the change and then after. Also explain the reasons the change occurred. (You may wish to look again at paragraphs 5–9 of "Halfway to Dick and Jane.")

Thoughts While Putting on Mascara Before Giving a Keynote Address

Anne Barrett Swanson

Looking Forward

Anne Barrett Swanson is an academic dean and a biochemist. The thoughts that she shares in this personal essay relate to the difficulties that she experiences because of her "differences": She is three feet seven inches and walks with a cane.

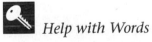 *Help with Words*

contours *(paragraph 1):* the outline of a figure, especially one that curves

function *(paragraph 2):* the activity for which a space is particularly fitted

compatriots *(paragraph 2):* colleagues

access codes *(paragraph 2):* legal requirements guaranteeing the handicapped equal rights to enter and use public places

juxtaposition *(paragraph 3):* placement of two things side by side, especially for comparison

preconceptions *(paragraph 3):* opinions arrived at before actual knowledge

aberrant *(paragraph 7):* different from the normal

I need a bit more blusher on my cheekbones. Last week at the 1
teacher's convention, it didn't matter as much. But tonight my
audience is a group of architects, and architects probably notice
contours and construction, even in the face. Will I be successful?
Will I be able to shift their awareness, ever so gradually, from the
way I look and the construction of my body, my legs and my cane,
to the construction of their buildings and their spaces?

Spaces, full of clean lines and light and function, but not for me 2
and my compatriots, not when some of us can't get in the door. The
access codes, they will say, are for public places but not for laboratories and workstations. The codes are for hospital rooms so we can
be good patients, but those codes need not apply to the medical labs
because that's where productive people do important work.

So until there are access codes and laws for those places where 3
we want to learn and work, I must rely on my words and my face.
And on my audience's surprise at the juxtaposition of my reality
with their preconceptions about disabled people.

Green eyeshadow will add a little drama. I remember what Rob 4
said about times like this: "You're on the chicken salad circuit now.
Don't forget to call me and tell me when you know you've batted
1,000 that day." Some days I did, and some days I didn't, but I usually called Rob anyway. Rob was one of the earliest fighters for our
cause, and he knew how important that phone call was to remind
me of the team out there pulling for me. You died way too soon,
Rob. Maybe it was too much chicken salad.

I'd better touch up that mascara on my left eye. I really should get 5
the waterproof kind. Once, at a scientists' meeting, I met a woman
in a sensible suit. She raked me over the coals for wearing makeup
and a flowing skirt and a long red silk scarf around my neck. She
said I was broadcasting that I was a woman, not a scientist, and if I
got more secure and embraced the women's movement, I would
stop dressing in such a silly way to attract the attention of men.

Such strange bedfellows we are, the women's movement and this 6
cause of ours which is emerging as a disability rights movement.
The women of my cause are struggling to be recognized as capable
and smart, and powerful, and not helpless, just as the woman in the
sensible suit was.

But we are also struggling to be acknowledged as women, to be   7
part of the human family, and sensual and attractive, no matter the
construction of our bodies; to be considered okay, not aberrant, if
we are wives and moms. The woman in the sensible suit was fighting against being forced to be those very things that we are fighting
for the right to become.

Just a little gloss over my lipstick and then I'm done. On the   8
chicken salad circuit, what is more powerful, my words or my face?
To speak words of power to these architects tonight, or to twinkle
and laugh at my own jokes, flaunt my new dress and put them at
ease with this alien who will show them she really is a member of
their family after all?

Fifteen minutes are left before the pre-conference reception be-   9
gins. I'll go downstairs early and make sure the hotel convention
manager put in that lowered podium I asked for, and check whether
I can easily climb the platform. Maybe I'll bat 1,000 with the architects tonight. If I do, Rob, I'll call you.

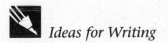 *A Second Look*

1 At what point in the essay is it clear that the author is physically
   handicapped?
2 Restate in your own words the exact point that Swanson hopes her
   speech to the architects will make. Why does she apply makeup to reen-
   force her speech?
3 The writer uses the application of her makeup to give order to her essay.
   Identify the paragraphs with references to makeup, and describe how
   these references contribute to the overall organization of the essay.
4 Makeup is also used to clarify the point that Swanson is making about
   the differences between the women's rights movement and the disability rights movement. What are some of these differences?

Ideas for Writing

Find out what is done on your campus to ensure equal access for physically handicapped students. You might consult the college catalog, student
handbook, or other school publications. Learn who is chiefly responsible

for ensuring equal access or find who on the staff counsels handicapped students, and interview those people. If you know handicapped students in your classes or your dorm, ask questions of them. When you have collected enough information, write an essay in which you tell what your school has done to guarantee equal access and indicate what further steps need to be taken.

On Being Seventeen, Bright, and Unable to Read

David Raymond

Looking Forward

David Raymond's difference is his inability to read—not because of any lack of training but because of dyslexia. This condition, which prevents a person from recognizing words and sometimes even numbers, results from a brain dysfunction. As Raymond's title suggests, dyslexia is unrelated to intelligence. Notice that Raymond opens with a specific example and then introduces his main idea in paragraph 2.

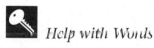 Help with Words

facilities *(paragraph 14):* places or equipment designed for special purposes

One day a substitute teacher picked me to read aloud from the textbook. When I told her, "No, thank you," she came unhinged. She thought I was acting smart, and told me so. I kept calm, and that got her madder and madder. We must have spent ten minutes trying to solve the problem, and finally she got so red in the face I thought she'd blow up. She told me she'd see me after class. 1

Maybe someone like me was a new thing for that teacher. But she 2
wasn't new to me. I've been through scenes like that all my life. You
see, even though I'm seventeen and a junior in high school, I can't
read because I have dyslexia. I'm told I read "at a fourth-grade
level," but from where I sit, that's not reading. You can't know what
that means unless you've been there. It's not easy to tell how it feels
when you can't read your homework assignments or the newspaper
or a menu in a restaurant or even notes from your own friends.

My family began to suspect I was having problems almost from 3
the first day I started school. My father says my early years in school
were the worst years of his life. They weren't so good for me, either.
As I look back on it now, I can't find the words to express how bad it
really was. I wanted to die. I'd come home from school screaming,
"I'm dumb. I'm dumb—I wish I were dead!"

I guess I couldn't read anything at all then—not even my own 4
name—and they tell me I didn't talk as good as other kids. But what
I remember about those days is that I couldn't throw a ball where it
was supposed to go, I couldn't learn to swim, and I wouldn't learn
to ride a bike, because no matter what anyone told me, I knew I'd
fail.

Sometimes my teachers would try to be encouraging. When I 5
couldn't read the words on the board they'd say, "Come on, David,
you know that word." Only I didn't. And it was embarrassing. I just
felt dumb. And dumb was how the kids treated me. They'd make
fun of me every chance they got, asking me to spell "cat" or something like that. Even if I knew how to spell it, I wouldn't; they'd only
give me another word. Anyway, it was awful, because more than
anything I wanted friends. On my birthday when I blew out the
candles I didn't wish I could learn to read; what I wished for was
that the kids would like me.

With the bad reports coming from school, and with me moaning 6
about wanting to die and how everybody hated me, my parents
began looking for help. That's when the testing started. The school
tested me, the child guidance center tested me, private psychiatrists
tested me. Everybody knew something was wrong—especially me.

It didn't help much when they stuck a fancy name onto it. I 7
couldn't pronounce it then—I was only in second grade—and I was
ashamed to talk about it. Now it rolls off my tongue, because I've
been living with it for a lot of years—dyslexia.

All through elementary school it wasn't easy. I was always hav- 8
ing to do things that were "different," things the other kids didn't
have to do. I had to go to a child psychiatrist, for instance.

One summer my family forced me to go to a camp for children 9
with reading problems. I hated the idea, but the camp turned out
pretty good, and I had a good time. I met a lot of kids who couldn't
read and somehow that helped. The director of the camp said I had
a higher IQ than 90 percent of the population. I didn't believe him.

About the worst thing I had to do in fifth and sixth grade was go 10
to a special education class in another school in our town. A bus
picked me up, and I didn't like that at all. The bus also picked up
emotionally disturbed kids and retarded kids. It was like going to a
school for the retarded. I always worried that someone I knew
would see me on that bus. It was a relief to go to the regular junior
high school.

Life began to change for me then, because I began to feel better 11
about myself. I found the teachers cared; they had meetings about
me and I worked harder for them for a while. I began to work on the
potter's wheel, making vases and pots that the teachers said were
pretty good. Also, I got a letter for being on the track team. I could
always run pretty fast.

At high school the teachers are good and everyone is trying to 12
help me. I've gotten honors some marking periods and I've won a
letter on the cross-country team. Next quarter I think the school
might hold a show of my pottery. I've got some friends. But there
are still some embarrassing times. For instance, every time there is
writing in the class, I get up and go to the special education room.
Kids ask me where I go all the time. Sometimes I say "To Mars."

Homework is a real problem. During free periods in school I go 13
into the special ed room and staff members read assignments to me.
When I get home my mother reads to me. Sometimes she reads an
assignment into a tape recorder and then I go into my room and
listen to it. If we have a novel or something like that to read, she
reads it out loud to me. Then I sit down with her and we do the
assignment. She'll write, while I talk my answers to her. Lately, I've
taken to dictating into a tape recorder, and then someone—my father, a private tutor or my mother—types up what I've dictated.
Whatever homework I do takes someone else's time, too. That
makes me feel bad.

We had a big meeting in school the other day—eight of us, four   14
from the guidance department, my private tutor, my parents and
me. The subject was me. I said I wanted to go to college, and they
told me about colleges that have facilities and staff to handle people
like me. That's nice to hear.

As for what happens after college, I don't know and I'm worried   15
about that. How can I make a living if I can't read? Who will hire
me? How will I fill out the application form?

The only thing that gives me any courage is the fact that I've   16
learned about well-known people who couldn't read or had other
problems and still made it. Like Albert Einstein, who didn't talk
until he was four and flunked math. Like Leonardo da Vinci, who
everyone seems to think had dyslexia.

I've told this story because maybe some teacher will read it and   17
go easy on a kid in the classroom who has what I've got. Or maybe
some parent will stop nagging his kid, and stop calling him lazy.
Maybe he's not lazy or dumb. Maybe he just can't read and doesn't
know what's wrong. Maybe he's scared, like I was.

 *A Second Look*

1 Besides the inability to read, what were some other early signs of David
   Raymond's dyslexia?
2 Mention several changes that helped Raymond feel better about himself.
3 Raymond often uses casual words or even slang—for example, "thought
   she'd blow up" (paragraph 1). Find other examples of this type of language. What impression does this language create?
4 Raymond uses many details from his personal experience. How does he
   put them in order?
5 In general, this essay explains what has happened to the writer and how
   he feels about it. The last paragraph, however, serves a different purpose. What is it?

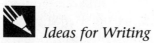 *Ideas for Writing*

1 Think of a time when you felt different from those around you. What
   was the difference? Did you look different or talk differently? Could

everyone else do something that you could not? As exactly as you can, remember the situation, and recall how you reacted. Were you embarrassed, angry, hurt, or all these?

Now write an essay in which you first describe the time when you felt different; then explain why you felt as you did. Finally, tell how you reacted. You will be writing, as David Raymond did, for a group of readers who do not know you.

2. One way of defining something is to explain how it works. David Raymond helps explain what dyslexia is by showing how it affected his life. If you know of some condition like dyslexia that has made a difference in your life or the life of someone you know, help define or explain that condition by showing its effects. You may begin, as Raymond did, with an example, or you may begin by mentioning the condition. Your readers may be familiar with the condition you are explaining, but they do not know you or the person you are writing about.

Harrison Bergeron

Kurt Vonnegut, Jr.

Looking Forward

Kurt Vonnegut, Jr., has been popular, especially with college-age readers, for a number of years. He has written many essays and short stories, in addition to such well-known novels as *Slaughterhouse Five* and *Breakfast of Champions*. In "Harrison Bergeron," a science fiction short story, Vonnegut imagines a future society in which all differences have been outlawed and the government is responsible for making everyone equal. Consider whether the government has completely succeeded and whether or not such equality is desirable.

Help with Words

unceasing vigilance *(paragraph 1):* endless watchfulness

sashweights *(paragraph 10):* weights used for raising and lowering windows

winced *(paragraph 11):* flinched or drew back slightly, as from pain

glimmeringly *(paragraph 21):* faintly

impediment *(paragraph 37):* handicap

luminous *(paragraph 41):* bright, glowing

grackle *(paragraph 42):* a bird with a harsh call

calibrated *(paragraph 43):* measured off

symmetry *(paragraph 45):* balance or order

consternation *(paragraph 49):* alarm or dismay

cowered *(paragraph 53):* knelt fearfully

capered *(paragraph 73):* leaped

gamboled *(paragraph 73):* skipped

Threw he year was 2081, and everybody was finally equal. They
weren't only equal before God and the law. They were equal
in every which way. Nobody was smarter than anybody else. Nobody was better looking than anybody else. Nobody was stronger
or quicker than anybody else. All this equality was due to the 211th,
212th, and 213th Amendments to the Constitution, and to the unceasing vigilance of agents of the United States Handicapper
General.

Some things about living still weren't quite right, though. April,
for instance, still drove people crazy by not being springtime. And it
was in that clammy month that the H-G men took George and Hazel Bergeron's fourteen-year-old son, Harrison, away.

It was tragic, all right, but George and Hazel couldn't think about
it very hard. Hazel had a perfectly average intelligence, which
meant she couldn't think about anything except in short bursts.
And George, while his intelligence was way above normal, had a
little mental handicap radio in his ear. He was required by law to
wear it at all times. It was tuned to a government transmitter. Every
twenty seconds or so, the transmitter would send out some sharp
noise to keep people like George from taking unfair advantage of
their brains.

George and Hazel were watching television. There were tears on
Hazel's cheeks, but she'd forgotten for the moment what they were
about.

On the television screen were ballerinas.

A buzzer sounded in George's head. His thoughts fled in panic,
like bandits from a burglar alarm.

"That was a real pretty dance, that dance they just did," said
Hazel.

"Huh?" said George.

"That dance—it was nice," said Hazel.

"Yup," said George. He tried to think a little about the ballerinas.
They weren't really very good—no better than anybody else would
have been anyway. They were burdened with sashweights and bags
of birdshot, and their faces were masked, so that no one, seeing a
free and graceful gesture or a pretty face, would feel like something

the cat drug in. George was toying with the vague notion that maybe dancers shouldn't be handicapped. But he didn't get very far with it before another noise in his ear radio scattered his thoughts.

George winced. So did two out of the eight ballerinas. 11

Hazel saw him wince. Having no mental handicap herself, she had to ask George what the latest sound had been. 12

"Sounded like somebody hitting a milk bottle with a ball peen hammer," said George. 13

"I'd think it would be real interesting, hearing all the different sounds," said Hazel, a little envious. "All the things they think up." 14

"Um," said George. 15

"Only, if I was Handicapper General, you know what I would do?" said Hazel. Hazel, as a matter of fact, bore a strong resemblance to the Handicapper General, a woman named Diana Moon Glampers. "If I was Diana Moon Glampers," said Hazel, "I'd have chimes on Sunday—just chimes. Kind of in honor of religion." 16

"I could think, if it was just chimes," said George. 17

"Well—maybe make 'em real loud," said Hazel. "I think I'd make a good Handicapper General." 18

"Good as anybody else," said George. 19

"Who knows better'n I do what normal is?" said Hazel. 20

"Right," said George. He began to think glimmeringly about his abnormal son who was now in jail, about Harrison, but a twenty-one-gun salute in his head stopped that. 21

"Boy!" said Hazel, "that was a doozy, wasn't it?" 22

It was such a doozy that George was white and trembling, and tears stood on the rims of his red eyes. Two of the eight ballerinas had collapsed to the studio floor, were holding their temples. 23

"All of a sudden you look so tired," said Hazel. "Why don't you stretch out on the sofa, so's you can rest your handicap bag on the pillows, honeybunch." She was referring to the forty-seven pounds of birdshot in a canvas bag, which was padlocked around George's neck. "Go on and rest the bag for a little while," she said. "I don't care if you're not equal to me for a while." 24

George weighed the bag with his hands. "I don't mind it," he said. "I don't notice it any more. It's just a part of me." 25

"You've been so tired lately—kind of wore out," said Hazel. "If there was just some way we could make a little hole in the bottom of the bag, and just take out a few of them lead balls, just a few." 26

"Two years in prison and two thousand dollars fine for every ball 27
I took out," said George. "I don't call that a bargain."

"If you could just take a few out when you came home from 28
work," said Hazel. "I mean—you don't compete with anybody
around here. You just set around."

"If I tried to get away with it," said George, "then other people'd 29
get away with it—and pretty soon we'd be right back to the dark
ages again, with everybody competing against everybody else. You
wouldn't like that, would you?"

"I'd hate it," said Hazel. 30

"There you are," said George. "The minute people start cheating 31
on laws, what do you think happens to society?"

If Hazel hadn't been able to come up with an answer to this ques- 32
tion, George couldn't have supplied one. A siren was going off in
his head.

"Reckon it'd fall all apart," said Hazel. 33

"What would?" said George blankly. 34

"Society," said Hazel uncertainly. "Wasn't that what you just said?" 35

"Who knows?" said George. 36

The television program was suddenly interrupted for a news bul- 37
letin. It wasn't clear at first as to what the bulletin was about, since
the announcer, like all announcers, had a serious speech impediment. For about half a minute, and in a state of high excitement, the
announcer tried to say, "Ladies and gentlemen—"

He finally gave up, handed the bulletin to a ballerina to read. 38

"That's all right—" Hazel said to the announcer, "he tried. That's 39
the big thing. He tried to do the best he could with what God gave
him. He should get a nice raise for trying so hard."

"Ladies and gentlemen—" said the ballerina, reading the bulle- 40
tin. She must have been extraordinarily beautiful because the mask
she wore was hideous. And it was easy to see that she was the
strongest and most graceful of all the dancers, for her handicap bags
were as big as those worn by two-hundred-pound men.

And she had to apologize at once for her voice, which was a very 41
unfair voice for a woman to use. Her voice was warm, luminous,
timeless, melody. "Excuse me—" she said, and she began again,
making her voice absolutely uncompetitive.

"Harrison Bergeron, age fourteen," she said in a grackle squawk, 42
"has just escaped from jail, where he was held on suspicion of plot-

ting to overthrow the government. He is a genius and an athlete, is underhandicapped, and should be regarded as extremely dangerous."

A police photograph of Harrison Bergeron was flashed on the 43 screen upside down, then sideways, upside down again, then right side up. The picture showed the full length of Harrison against a background calibrated in feet and inches. He was exactly seven feet tall.

The rest of Harrison's appearance was Halloween and hardware. 44 Nobody had ever borne heavier handicaps. He had outgrown hindrances faster than the H-G men could think them up. Instead of a little ear radio for a mental handicap, he wore a tremendous pair of earphones, and spectacles with thick wavy lenses. The spectacles were intended to make him not only half blind, but to give him whanging headaches besides.

Scrap metal was hung all over him. Ordinarily, there was a cer- 45 tain symmetry, a military neatness to the handicaps issued to strong people, but Harrison looked like a walking junkyard. In the race of life, Harrison carried three hundred pounds.

And to offset his good looks, H-G men required that he wear at all 46 times a red rubber ball for a nose, keep his eyebrows shaved off, and cover his even white teeth with black caps at snaggletooth random.

"If you see this boy," said the ballerina, "do not—I repeat, do 47 not—try to reason with him."

There was the shriek of a door being torn from its hinges. 48

Screams and barking cries of consternation came from the televi- 49 sion set. The photograph of Harrison Bergeron on the screen jumped again and again, as though dancing to the tune of an earthquake.

George Bergeron correctly identified the earthquake, and well he 50 might have—for many was the time his own home had danced to the same crashing tune. "My God—" said George, "that must be Harrison!"

The realization was blasted from his mind instantly by the sound 51 of an automobile collision in his head.

When George could open his eyes again, the photograph of Har- 52 rison was gone. A living, breathing Harrison filled the screen.

Clanking, clownish, and huge, Harrison stood in the center of the 53 studio. The knob of the uprooted studio door was still in his hand. Ballerinas, technicians, musicians, and announcers cowered on their knees before him, expecting to die.

"I am the Emperor!" cried Harrison. "Do you hear? I am the Emperor! Everybody must do what I say at once!" He stamped his foot and the studio shook.   54

"Even as I stand here—" he bellowed, "crippled, hobbled, sickened—I am a greater ruler than any man who ever lived! Now watch me become what I *can* become!"   55

Harrison tore the straps of his handicap harness like wet tissue paper, tore straps guaranteed to support five thousand pounds.   56

Harrison's scrap-iron handicaps crashed to the floor.   57

Harrison thrust his thumbs under the bar of the padlock that secured his head harness. The bar snapped like celery. Harrison smashed his headphones and spectacles against the wall.   58

He flung away his rubber-ball nose, revealed a man that would have awed Thor, the god of thunder.   59

"I shall now select my Empress!" he said, looking down on the cowering people. "Let the first woman who dares rise to her feet claim her mate and her throne!"   60

A moment passed, and then a ballerina arose, swaying like a willow.   61

Harrison plucked the mental handicap from her ear, snapped off her physical handicaps with marvelous delicacy. Last of all, he removed her mask.   62

She was blindingly beautiful.   63

"Now—" said Harrison, taking her hand, "shall we show the people the meaning of the word dance? Music!" he commanded.   64

The musicians scrambled back into their chairs, and Harrison stripped them of their handicaps, too. "Play your best," he told them, "and I'll make you barons and dukes and earls."   65

The music began. It was normal at first—cheap, silly, false. But Harrison snatched two musicians from their chairs, waved them like batons as he sang the music as he wanted it played. He slammed them back into their chairs.   66

The music began again and was much improved.   67

Harrison and his Empress merely listened to the music for a while—listened gravely, as though synchronizing their heartbeats with it.   68

They shifted their weights to their toes.   69

Harrison placed his big hand on the girl's tiny waist, letting her sense the weightlessness that would soon be hers.   70

And then, in an explosion of joy and grace, into the air they 71
sprang!

Not only were the laws of the land abandoned, but the law of 72
gravity and the laws of motion as well.

They reeled, whirled, swiveled, flounced, capered, gamboled, 73
and spun.

They leaped like deer on the moon. 74

The studio ceiling was thirty feet high, but each leap brought the 75
dancers nearer to it.

It became their obvious intention to kiss the ceiling. 76

They kissed it. 77

And then, neutralizing gravity with love and pure will, they re- 78
mained suspended in air inches below the ceiling, and they kissed
each other for a long, long time.

It was then that Diana Moon Glampers, the Handicapper Gen- 79
eral, came into the studio with a double-barreled 10-gauge shotgun.
She fired twice, and the Emperor and Empress were dead before
they hit the floor.

Diana Moon Glampers loaded the gun again. She aimed it at the 80
musicians and told them they had ten seconds to get their handicaps back on.

It was then that the Bergeron's television tube burned out. 81

Hazel turned to comment about the blackout to George. But 82
George had gone out into the kitchen for a can of beer.

George came back in with the beer, paused while a handicap sig- 83
nal shook him up. And then he sat down again. "You been crying?"
he said to Hazel.

"Yup," she said. 84

"What about?" he said. 85

"I forget," she said. "Something real sad on television." 86

"What was it?" he said. 87

"It's all kind of mixed up in my mind," said Hazel. 88

"Forget sad things," said George. 89

"I always do," said Hazel. 90

"That's my girl," said George. He winced. There was the sound 91
of a riveting gun in his head.

"Gee—I could tell that one was a doozy," said Hazel. 92

"You can say that again," said George. 93

"Gee—" said Hazel, "I could tell that one was a doozy." 94

A Second Look

1 How are George and Hazel different from each other?

2 Describe the kinds of handicaps George has been given.

3 In paragraph 14, we learn that Hazel is "a little envious." Why? What does this suggest about the plan for universal equality?

4 How is Diana Moon Glampers, the Handicapper General, different from everyone else in the story?

5 Vonnegut certainly does not believe that such "equality" is good. Point out several places where he suggests that this idea is unworkable.

6 What words in paragraphs 69–71 suggest movement? Why is movement so important at this point in the story?

7 Define equality, as Vonnegut describes it in the story. What is your definition of the term?

Ideas for Writing

1 Reread paragraphs 66–79, which describe the scene in the TV studio just as the Handicapper General arrives and then her response to that scene. Try to imagine this action from the Handicapper General's point of view. Write a brief, factual report from the Handicapper General to the President, explaining (from her point of view) what was occurring and what action she had to take.

2 Imagine how some one part of society or one type of common experience may differ in 2081. You might choose law enforcement, marriage, factory work, teaching and learning, or any activity about which your imagination can roam. If your instructor wishes, you might brainstorm in small groups of three or four. In your brainstorming session, think of as many details as possible about the way your activity will be carried out in 2081. Then select those that are most interesting or that best go together to make a complete description. (You may do this individually, or if you are working in groups, you may discuss your list with others.)

   When you write, you may assume that you are in the present predicting what the future will be like. In that case, you will write in the future tense. On the other hand, you could assume that you are already in the future and are describing what it is like. In that case, you will write in the present tense. (You might try the first paragraph both ways and see which you prefer.)

Making Connections

Jack Agueros, Anne Barrett Swanson, and David Raymond write about differences that can lead to discrimination. Kurt Vonnegut, Jr., presents differences as important and desirable. Do differences among people have a positive effect on society? When and how do differences cause social problems?

Sports

Head Down

Stephen King

Looking Forward

In this excerpt from a longer article, Stephen King takes a close look at a few very important moments for a group of preteen boys: the closing minutes of a Little League championship game. Bangor West is playing Hampden for the Penobscot County (Maine) title. It is now the bottom of the last inning. Hampden leads 14 to 12; Bangor West is at bat.

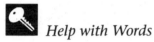 *Help with Words*

Hampden Horns *(parugraph 2):* Hampden fans who blow automobile and truck horns to cheer their players and intimidate the opposition
silhouettes *(paragraph 8):* outlines

L ast call for Bangor West. Jeff Carson, whose fourth-inning   1 home run is really the difference in this game, and who earlier replaced Mike Wentworth on the mound for Hampden, is now replaced by Mike Tardif. He faces Owen King first. King goes three and two (swinging wildly for the fences at one pitch in the dirt), then lays off a pitch just inside to work a walk. Roger Fisher follows him to the plate, pinch-hitting for . . . Fred Moore. Roger is a small boy, with Indian-dark eyes and hair. He looks like an easy out, but looks can be deceptive; Roger has good power. Today, however, he is overmatched. He strikes out.

In the field, the Hampden players shift around and look at each other. They are close, and they know it. The parking lot is too far away here for the Hampden Horns to be a factor; their fans settle for simply screaming encouragement. Two women wearing purple Hampden caps are standing behind the dugout, hugging each other joyfully. Several other fans look like track runners waiting for the starter's gun; it is clear they mean to rush onto the field the moment their boys succeed in putting Bangor West away for good. 2

Joe Wilcox, who didn't want to be a catcher and ended up doing the job anyway, rams a one-out single up the middle and into left center field. King stops at second. Up steps Arthur Dorr, the Bangor right fielder, who wears the world's oldest pair of high-top sneakers and has not had a hit all day. This time, he hits a shot, but right at the Hampden shortstop, who barely has to move. The shortstop whips the ball to second, hoping to catch King off the bag, but he's out of luck. Nevertheless, there are two out. 3

The Hampden fans scream further encouragement. The women behind the dugout are jumping up and down. Now there are a few Hampden Horns tootling away someplace, but they are a little early, and all one has to do to know it is to look at Mike Tardif's face as he wipes off his forehead and pounds the baseball into his glove. 4

Ryan Iarrobino steps into the right-hand batter's box. He has a fast, almost naturally perfect swing. . . . 5

Ryan swings through Tardif's first pitch, his hardest of the day— it makes a rifle-shot sound as it hits Kyle King's glove. Tardif then wastes one outside. King returns the ball, Tardif meditates briefly, and then throws a low fastball. Ryan looks at it, and the umpire calls strike two. It has caught the outside corner—maybe. The ump says it did, anyway, and that's the end of it. 6

Now the fans on both sides have fallen quiet, and so have the coaches. They're all out of it. It's only Tardif and Iarrobino now, balanced on the last strike of the last out of the last game one of these teams will play. Forty-six feet between these two faces. Only, Iarrobino is not watching Tardif's face. He is watching Tardif's glove. . . . 7

Iarrobino is waiting to see how Tardif will come. As Tardif moves to the set position, you can faintly hear the pock-pock, pock-pock of tennis balls on a nearby court, but here there is only silence and the crisp black shadows of the players, lying on the dirt like silhouettes 8 cut from black construction paper, and Iarrobino is waiting to see how Tardif will come.

He comes over the top. And suddenly Iarrobino is in motion, both knees and the left shoulder dipping slightly, the aluminum bat a blur in the sunlight. That aluminum-on-cowhide sound—*chink*, like someone hitting a tin cup with a spoon—is different this time. A *lot* different. Not *chink* but *crunch* as Ryan connects, and then the ball is in the sky, tracking out to left field—a long shot that is clearly gone, high, wide, and handsome into the summer afternoon. The ball will later be recovered from beneath a car about two hundred and seventy-five feet away from home plate.

The expression on twelve-year-old Mike Tardif's face is stunned, thunderstruck disbelief. He takes one quick look into his glove, as if hoping to find the ball still there and discover that Iarrobino's dramatic two-strike, two-out shot was only a hideous momentary dream. The two women behind the backstop look at each other in total amazement. At first, no one makes a sound. In that moment before everyone begins to scream and the Bangor West players rush out of their dugout to await Ryan at home plate and mob him when he arrives, only two people are entirely sure that it did really happen. One is Ryan himself. As he rounds first, he raises both hands to his shoulders in a brief but emphatic gesture of triumph. And, as Owen King crosses the plate with the first of the three runs that will end Hampden's All-Star season, Mike Tardif realizes. Standing on the pitcher's rubber for the last time as a Little Leaguer, he bursts into tears.

A Second Look

1 King's description causes the reader to take a genuine interest in these young players. How does he make them real people and not merely names?

2 What details help us sense the tension felt by both players and spectators in these closing minutes?

3 What change does King make in his description in paragraphs 7–9? Do you think the change is effective?

4 Why do you think King closes by focusing on the losing pitcher, not the winning runners?

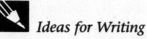 *Ideas for Writing*

1   Describe the winning or losing minutes of a competition in which you participated. (This may be a sports event, but it does not have to be. It could be a speech contest, an academic or musical competition, and so forth.) As King did, use specific details to make the readers feel as if they are there with you. List every detail you can think of related to this experience; as you write, select those that seem most important or fit best into your description.

2   Many people believe that through athletic competition children learn lessons about success and failure that will help them later in life. Tell about an experience in which you or someone you know learned such a lesson.

We Are the Best

Mariah Burton Nelson

Looking Forward

Susan Butcher has competed in the Iditarod Trail Sled Dog Race since 1978, and she has won the race, which covers a frozen 1,049-mile gold rush route, four times since 1988. Butcher usually does not think about her role as a woman dogsled racer competing with men; she loves the sport and wants to win no matter whom she defeats. However, as Mariah Burton Nelson points out, others cannot fail to look at her example with pride. She, along with the other women who have competed and won against men, has shown that women can be the best of all.

Help with Words

grueling *(paragraph 3):* exhausting, strenuous

introspection *(paragraph 4):* self-analysis

vicariously *(paragraph 8):* felt or enjoyed through imagined participation

amassed *(paragraph 9):* accumulated

marauding *(paragraph 10):* wandering to look for food

unprecedented *(paragraph 10):* never known before

leery *(paragraph 12):* wary, cautious

ascendancy *(paragraph 15):* mastery, power

public domain *(paragraph 18):* area owned by the public at large

notoriety *(paragraph 18):* fame

simultaneously *(paragraph 19):* occurring at the same time

inveterate *(paragraph 21):* constant

T o play with men is one thing. To defeat men is something   1
else entirely.

Susan Butcher has defeated boys since she was a little girl grow-   2
ing up in Cambridge, Massachusetts. Canoeing, sailing, running,
mountain climbing: she was always the best. Not the best in the
women's division, the best of all.

Eventually she made defeating men a career, although she   3
doesn't think of it that way. Because of her love of dogs, snow, cold,
wilderness, competition, and adventure, she became an Alaskan
dogsled racer, competing each year since 1978 in the Iditarod Trail
Sled Dog Race, a grueling eleven- or twelve-day, 1,049-mile trek
from Anchorage to Nome along an old route of the Alaskan gold
rush. For three years in a row, from 1986 to 1988, and again in 1990,
Butcher won the race. She didn't win the women's division—there
isn't such a thing—she won the race.

It's nothing personal, this beating-men thing. Susan doesn't see it   4
as anything with deep psychological significance. She doesn't trace
her competitiveness to her father, who, before divorcing her
mother, taught Susan and her sister to sail and ski. She doesn't say,
as many women do, that her father wanted a boy. Analysis and
introspection are distasteful to her. That's one thing she likes about
living in the Alaskan bush: people are too busy working to spend
time sitting around thinking about things.

"I'm lucky to have grown up feeling there were no restrictions on   5
me because I was a woman," Susan says. Does it have any particular relevance to her, then, that for five years she has dominated a
sport that includes men as well as women? "Oh, it has tons of relevance. It's more of a challenge. I enjoy it. From the time I was a little
tiny girl, I was the first girl to do this or the first girl to do that. At
coed camps I would better all the boys."

What's so great about beating boys?   6

"I don't know," she says. "I was just trying to beat everybody, I   7
guess. And that included the men."

This is how men get to feel—a few men, for a few moments, and   8
all men, vicariously: the best. Not the best of one gender, but the
best of all.

At this moment in history, the sports in which the best women are most likely to equal or exceed the best men are those that require flexibility or endurance or those in which horses, dogs, cars, go-carts, guns, or other machines or animals are involved. Susan Butcher came to this realization in her late teens, and it was upsetting. The boys she had been beating in every conceivable endeavor miraculously grew taller than she did and amassed muscles that dwarfed hers. If you want to be the best person, adolescence can be a drag. "Sure, I could still beat a lot of them in arm wrestling and things like that, but in all-out speed, I couldn't," she remembers. "Endurance I've always had, so in mountain climbing I could still be one of the very best people. I didn't pick it for that reason, but I was lucky to end up with a sport [dogsled racing] where I'm able to compete on an equal level." . . .

Male dogsled racers have had more time than squash players to get used to coed competition. Women have been racing in the Iditarod since 1974, its second year, and from one to ten women enter each year in an average field of fifty-three racers. Susan Butcher was the first woman to place in the top twenty, the first woman to place in the top ten, the first woman to place in the top five, and the first woman to finish second. Libby Riddles was the first woman to win; that was 1985, the year a marauding moose attacked Susan's team, killing two of her dogs and injuring several others. So by 1986, when Susan began her unprecedented (by women or men) three-year winning streak, the men in the race had heard plenty of times about this "first woman" to do this and that.

"Tell me how men have responded to you," I say to Susan. "You must have stories."

"I'm leery of telling them," she answers. "There are some wonderful men who love the fact that I'm doing what I'm doing and that I'm a woman. Then there are the even better ones who don't even notice that I'm a woman. They are very respectful of my ability as a dog musher.

"Then there's the norm. Because the media has put so much attention on the fact that I'm a woman, men resent that. They get pretty sick of 'Are you guys ever going to win this race again?' But also, there's a jovial sort of, 'Oh, we can't let Susan win again, we've got to get it back.'"

There is a lot of ground to cover here, there are a lot of men in her life. She pauses, as if coming to a brief rest stop at the end of a snowfield. Then she takes off again. "In the beginning there did seem to be a we-and-you situation where I was the only woman running in the top pack. There seemed to be such a buddy system among them, and I was not included. Now that I'm winning, there are some who are very seriously against me, more so than if I were a male champion. I pay little attention to it."

This "pay them no mind" strategy is a deliberate, practiced one.   15 "When I ran into blockades, I didn't look at them," she says of her ascendancy to top dogsled racer. "I just went right through them. I was unaware that I was fighting a fight. When I would talk to some of my feminist friends and say, 'I've had it, I'm so sick and tired of it. Why is this happening?' they would say, 'Susan, a woman has never done what you're doing. You're hitting every wall.' There were so many men down on me, working against me in groups—yes, I felt it and knew it, but I didn't want to look at it. I'm not one to sit there and go, 'Boo-hoo, why are people doing this to me?' or ask for help from fellow women or the law or whatever.

"We don't need to be condemning men, we don't need to ask men   16 to move over. We're just there. We just have to do it now. I'm tired of the 'pity me, I've been oppressed' thing. I am not a pitiful person. I don't want [men] to move over and let me win the Iditarod. I want to win it on my own, fair and square. The fact that they sometimes team up against me makes it that much more of a challenge and gives what I do that much more credibility." . . .

Because Susan Butcher has become the best in the world at a   17 sport no one heard of until women started winning, women get to say, "We are the best." ("She won!" cyclist Elaine Mariolle excitedly told my answering machine when she heard that Susan had won the 1990 race, breaking her own record in a time of 11 days, 1 hour, 53 minutes. "I feel so wonderful!") No matter that still no one outside Alaska knows much about dogsled racing. . . . We won. We are the best. Or at least, we are the best too.

Women and girls need heroes, as Merrily Dean Baker, assistant   18 executive director of the NCAA, often says: female heroes. It's not so much that they need heroes who defeat men, but they need heroes who are successful in the larger world, in the public domain; women who climb mountains and drive fast cars and win notoriety and have adventures not in the Powder Puff league, but real adventures, where the adventurers are not defined by femaleness. *I'm*

*lucky to have grown up feeling there were no restrictions on me because I
was a woman.*

Women need Chris Evert, who showed them that they could play   19
sports and simultaneously play the feminine role, but they also
need Susan Butcher, who refuses to play any role. Just as her skin
tone and height are no big deal to her, not character-defining qualities, so it is with her femaleness. She happens to be a woman, happens to have brown hair. Now, where's the dogsled?

I tell my little neighbor, Lora Cary, about Susan Butcher's victo-   20
ries. The next day I'm spreading gravel in my driveway, assisted by
Lora and the boy next door, Jaimie Graham. "Lora, you can't push
the wheelbarrow, you're not strong enough," Jaimie tells Lora. Jaimie is a year older than Lora, and bigger. The son of a feminist,
Jaimie may be referring to Lora's relative size and youth, not her
gender. He knows that women are not weak.

No matter. Lora, an inveterate soccer player, has already heard   21
"You can't because you're a girl" so many times that she hears it
even when that's not what's being said. "Girls are just as good as
boys, Jaimie," she tells him. "Some are better. Like Susan Butcher."

Lora needs Susan Butcher as I needed Babe Didrikson Zaharias,   22
the only female athlete I knew about as a child. As role models go,
Susan is even better than Babe: she's not just good, for a girl—she's
good, period. She's the best of all. Therefore, Lora has a right to hold
the wheelbarrow. It's a giant leap from Alaska to a Virginia driveway but a small step in the mind of a nine-year-old girl.

A Second Look

1 What does Nelson mean when she says of Susan Butcher: "It's nothing
   personal, this beating-men thing" (paragraph 4)?
2 What enables Butcher to achieve greater success in the dogsled racing
   than she could in many other sports?
3 If you have read Catherine Ettlinger's "Skiing with the Guys," compare
   Ettlinger's attitude toward skiing with Butcher's toward racing. See especially paragraphs 14 and 16 of Nelson's essay.
4 What is the point of Nelson's concluding story about her young neighbor, Lora Cary?

Ideas for Writing

1 Do you have a "sports hero," either man or woman? If so, write an essay telling who this person is, what he or she has done that is beyond the ordinary, and why you admire him or her. What will interest your readers is not primarily biographical facts and sports statistics, though those may be important to include. What readers want most to know is why you personally would choose this individual as a sports hero.

2 One place where there has been a strong attempt to ensure equality among male and female athletes is in public schools and colleges. The major equalizer is Title IX of the 1972 Education Amendments. As is often the case with government policies, the language of Title IX sounds unexciting, even dull: "No person in the United States shall, on the basis of sex, be excluded from participation in, be denied the benefits of, or be subjected to discrimination under any education program or activity receiving federal financial assistance. . . ." Yet Title IX has been the subject of debate and legal action for twenty years now, and the dust— instead of settling—seems recently to have swirled up again.

Using periodical or newspaper indexes, locate and read several recent articles or news reports on the success of Title IX. Take notes as you read. Then write a paper summarizing the material you have found. Your instructor or a reference librarian can give you additional help in your library search.

Send Your Children to the Libraries

Arthur Ashe

Looking Forward

Arthur Ashe played professional tennis for a number of years, winning many awards. He was outstanding in both Wimbledon and Davis Cup competition. But in this letter published in *The New York Times*, Ashe argues that there are actually few opportunities in professional sports for black athletes. He suggests that there are many roles in society, besides those in sports, that blacks can and should fill.

 ### Help with Words

pretentious *(paragraph 2):* falsely superior
expends *(paragraph 3):* spends
dubious *(paragraph 3):* questionable
emulate *(paragraph 4):* follow or imitate
massive *(paragraph 6):* very large
viable *(paragraph 9):* workable
channel *(paragraph 12):* direct

Since my sophomore year at University of California, Los Angeles, I have become convinced that we blacks spend too much time on the playing fields and too little time in the libraries. 1

Please don't think of this attitude as being pretentious just because I am a black, single, professional athlete. 2

I don't have children, but I can make observations. I strongly 3
believe the black culture expends too much time, energy and effort
raising, praising and teasing our black children as to the dubious
glories of professional sports.

All children need models to emulate—parents, relatives or 4
friends. But when the child starts school, the influence of the parent
is shared by teachers and classmates, by the lure of books, movies,
ministers and newspapers, but most of all by television.

Which televised events have the greatest number of viewers? 5
Sports—the Olympics, Super Bowl, Masters, World Series, pro basketball playoffs, Forest Hills. ABC-TV even has sports on Monday
night prime time from April to December.

So your child gets a massive dose of O. J. Simpson, Kareem Ab- 6
dul-Jabbar, Muhammad Ali, Reggie Jackson, Dr. J. and Lee Elder
and other pro athletes. And it is only natural that your child will
dream of being a pro athlete himself.

But consider these facts: For the major professional sports of 7
hockey, football, basketball, baseball, golf, tennis and boxing, there
are roughly only 3,170 major league positions available (attributing
200 positions to golf, 200 to tennis and 100 to boxing). And the an-
nual turnover is small.

We blacks are a subculture of about 28 million. Of the 13½ million 8
men, 5–6 million are under twenty years of age, so your son has less
than one chance in a thousand of becoming a pro. Less than one in a
thousand. Would you bet your son's future on something with odds
of 999 to 1 against you? I wouldn't.

Unless a child is exceptionally gifted, you should know by the 9
time he enters high school whether he has a future as an athlete. But
what is more important is what happens if he doesn't graduate or
doesn't land a college scholarship and doesn't have a viable alterna-
tive job career. Our high school dropout rate is several times the
national average, which contributes to our unemployment rate of
roughly twice the national average.

And how do you fight the figures in the newspapers every day? 10
Ali has earned more than $30 million boxing, O. J. just signed for
$2½ million, Dr. J. for almost $3 million, Reggie Jackson for $2.8
million, Nate Archibald for $400,000 a year. All that money, recogni-
tion, attention, free cars, girls, jobs in the off-season—no wonder
there is Pop Warner football, Little League baseball, National Junior

League tennis, hockey practice at 5 A.M. and pickup basketball games in any center city at any hour.

There must be some way to assure that the 999 who try but don't 11 make it to pro sports don't wind up on the street corners or in the unemployment lines. Unfortunately, our most widely recognized role models are athletes and entertainers—"runnin'" and "jumpin'" and "singin'" and "dancin'." While we are 60 percent of the National Basketball Association, we are less than 4 percent of the doctors and lawyers. While we are about 35 percent of major league baseball, we are less than 2 percent of the engineers. While we are about 40 percent of the National Football League, we are less than 11 percent of construction workers such as carpenters and bricklayers.

Our greatest heroes of the century have been athletes—Jack 12 Johnson, Joe Louis and Muhammad Ali. Racial and economic discrimination forced us to channel our energies into athletics and entertainment. These were the ways out of the ghetto, the ways to that Cadillac, those alligator shoes, that cashmere sport coat.

Somehow, parents must instill a desire for learning alongside the 13 desire to be Walt Frazier. Why not start by sending black professional athletes to high schools to explain the facts of life.

I have often addressed high school audiences and my message is 14 always the same. For every hour you spend on the athletic field, spend two in the library. Even if you make it as a pro athlete, your career will be over by the time you are thirty-five. So you will need that diploma.

Have these pro athletes explain what happens if you break a leg, 15 get a sore arm, have one bad year or don't make the cut for five or six tournaments. Explain to them the star system, wherein for every O. J. earning millions there are six or seven others making $15,000 or $20,000 or $30,000 a year.

But don't just have Walt Frazier or O. J. or Abdul-Jabbar address 16 your class. Invite a benchwarmer or a guy who didn't make it. Ask him if he sleeps every night. Ask him whether he was graduated. Ask him what he would do if he became disabled tomorrow. Ask him where his old high school athletic buddies are.

We have been on the same roads—sports and entertainment— 17 too long. We need to pull over, fill up at the library and speed away to Congress and the Supreme Court, the unions and the business world. We need more Barbara Jordans, Andrew Youngs, union cardholders, Nikki Giovannis and Earl Graveses. Don't worry: We will still be able to sing and dance and run and jump better than anybody else.

I'll never forget how proud my grandmother was when I gradu- 18 ated from UCLA in 1966. Never mind the Davis Cup in 1968, 1969, and 1970. Never mind the Wimbledon title, Forest Hills, etc. To this day, she still doesn't know what those names mean.

What mattered to her was that of her more than thirty children 19 and grandchildren, I was the first to be graduated from college, and a famous college at that. Somehow, that made up for all those floors she scrubbed all those years.

AFTERWORD

Since Arthur Ashe first achieved world fame by winning the U.S. Open in 1968, he has spoken and written often about the importance—in fact, the necessity—of getting a good education. In early April, 1992, Ashe announced that he had tested positive for the AIDS virus. His doctors believe he was infected by a blood transfusion following heart surgery in 1983, two years before blood screening for HIV was required. Ashe revealed his condition reluctantly, not only because he valued his privacy but also because he feared that this news might overshadow the point he has emphasized for over twenty years.

An editorial writer for *The Miami Herald* summarizes and comments on the importance of Ashe's message this way:

> . . . The odds of a young athlete's becoming a big money star in pro sports are about as good as his chances of winning the lottery.
>
> It is essential, then, that he pursue an education with the same zeal as he pursues success in sports. That, essentially, is Ashe's message. He has worked tirelessly to deliver it to America's young people—especially to those minorities who often see athletics as the only available means of escaping poverty.
>
> Sometimes he's upstaged by the clatter and hype of big-money sports, but that doesn't make his message or his mission any less valid.
>
> Arthur Ashe still serves well.

A Second Look

1 In this letter, Ashe uses many statistics. Are they convincing? Why or why not?

2 What evidence besides statistics does he use to support his main idea?

3 Ashe says, in paragraph 17, "We have been on the same roads—sports and entertainment—too long." Does he mean that blacks should avoid these careers?

4 Ashe's audience consists of parents of black sons. Could his argument apply to other races or to parents of girls? Why or why not?

5 The best piece of evidence to strengthen Ashe's argument may be Ashe himself. How does the letter show this?

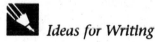 *Ideas for Writing*

Write a letter to the editor in which you state an opinion that you feel strongly about. Begin by stating the opinion clearly in a single sentence. Decide who your readers will be. Are you writing for a campus newspaper? A community newspaper? A big-city daily?

Next, write down all the reasons you can think of why your readers should accept your opinion. Decide which are most effective, and then begin to organize your letter. Begin with your statement of opinion. Follow with support. Near the end, restate the opinion though not in the same words you used at the beginning.

Ex-Basketball Player

John Updike

Looking Forward

Poet, novelist, and short story writer John Updike has often written about former athletes, like Flick Webb in this poem. In the poem, Updike shows how Flick's life has changed by describing him at work and after work. Pay special attention to Flick's feelings about his past.

 Help with Words

tiers *(line 29):* rows rising one behind the other, as in bleachers
Necco Wafers, Nibs, and Juju Beads *(line 30):* brands of candy and snacks

Pearl Avenue runs past the high school lot,   1
    Bends with the trolley tracks, and stops, cut off
Before it has a chance to go two blocks,
At Colonel McComsky Plaza. Berth's Garage
Is on the corner facing west, and there,   5
Most days, you'll find Flick Webb, who helps Berth out.

Flick stands tall among the idiot pumps—
Five on a side, the old bubble-head style,
Their rubber elbows hanging loose and low.
One's nostrils are two S's, and his eyes   10
An E and O. And one is squat, without
A head at all—more of a football type.

Once, Flick played for the high school team, the Wizards.
He was good: in fact, the best. In '46,
He bucketed three hundred ninety points,   15
A county record still. The ball loved Flick.
I saw him rack up thirty-eight or forty
In one home game. His hands were like wild birds.

He never learned a trade; he just sells gas,
Checks oil, and changes flats. Once in a while,   20
As a gag, he dribbles an inner tube,
But most of us remember anyway.
His hands are fine and nervous on the lug wrench.
It makes no difference to the lug wrench, though.

Off work, he hangs around Mae's Luncheonette.   25
Grease-grey and kind of coiled, he plays pinball,
Sips lemon cokes, and smokes those thin cigars;
Flick seldom speaks to Mae, just sits and nods
Beyond her face toward the bright applauding tiers
Of Necco Wafers, Nibs, and Juju Beads.   30

 A Second Look

1 Updike shows much about Flick's life by setting up comparisons. How
   does the description of Pearl Avenue apply to Flick? What is suggested
   by the description of the pumps?
2 What lines of the poem reveal Flick's talent?
3 What lines show that he lives mainly in the past?

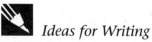 *Ideas for Writing*

1 Without using Updike's exact words, describe Flick Webb in a paragraph.
2 Have you known someone like Flick Webb, someone who lives on past
   glory achieved in any field? Describe this person. Tell your readers
   (who do not know your subject) what kind of success this person had
   and what kind of person he or she is now.

Making Connections

Stephen King and Mariah Burton Nelson present quite positive views of sports. Arthur Ashe and John Updike suggest some of the negative aspects. Referring to these selections and using your own knowledge, list the pluses and minuses of participation in sports on the amateur level. If your instructor wishes, you might work on this in small groups. Do the positives outweigh the negatives? Can some of the negatives be eliminated or at least neutralized?

Black Women
in the White House

Laura B. Randolph

Looking Forward

In this article from *Ebony*, Laura B. Randolph writes about three women
who found highly successful careers in the Bush White House. This selection profiles Anna Perez, Press Secretary to First Lady Barbara Bush.
Perez's success story shows what *can* happen—but too seldom *does* happen—in the "land of opportunity."

 Help with Words

ensconced *(paragraph 2):* settled securely
adversity *(paragraph 6):* hardship, bad luck
aberration *(paragraph 6):* unusual circumstance, abnormality
prominent *(paragraph 9):* famous, prestigious
unorthodox *(paragraph 10):* unusual, not generally accepted
intimidated *(paragraph 11):* frightened, overawed

Sweet satisfaction filled Anna Perez as she settled into her seat   1
on the first lady's Air Force jet. Even after more than a year as
Barbara Bush's chief spokesperson, Perez couldn't help marveling
at the rare and remarkable joys of her position.

Perez has good reason to be a little wide-eyed about her job of   2
representing the first lady's views to the press, the country, the

world. There was a time when she dreamed not of having a White House office, but a roof over her family's head. She may be firmly ensconced in the most prestigious address in the world, but Perez knows well the view from the other side.

When she was in the fifth grade, Perez came home from school 3 and found her family and all their belongings sitting on the street. It took her a few minutes to realize what had happened, but then she understood. Her mother, two older brothers and two younger sisters had been evicted. They were homeless.

"We were evicted from a lot of places we lived in," recalls the 4 New York-born Perez of the days immediately following her parents' break-up. "Things got very rough . . . my mom had to split up the family—my brothers and sisters went to live in Dallas with relatives; I lived with my fifth-grade teacher for a while and my mom stayed at a hotel for the homeless."

Now that she's settled in the West Wing office that once belonged 5 to Rosalyn Carter, the sweet irony of her journey is in no way lost on her. "I was sitting next to [pop singer] Paul Simon who has a wonderful program with medical vans that go around to homeless hotels in New York City, and it just struck me that here I am sitting next to Paul Simon at a benefit and he's helping the people who live in the same shelter that my family used to live in. Talk about coming full circle . . . ," she says surveying her domain and resting her gaze on a photo of her mom with a smiling Barbara Bush.

Looking back on those days now that she's a mother (son Anthony is 12, daughter Candace is 9 and stepdaughter Niambi, 17), 6 Perez says she can't imagine how her mom managed to keep up their spirits in the face of such adversity. "No matter how bad things got, my mother made it clear that this was an aberration. We were not defined by our financial situation. We were defined by our ability to overcome it."

Not even Perez expected she would overcome it quite so dramat- 7 ically. After leaving home at 18, she put herself through Hunter College by working as a governess, but dropped out after her junior year "because I was bored and wasn't getting that much out of it." She spent the next five years as a United Airlines flight attendant.

Restless again, she moved to California to work as a marketing 8 specialist and met her husband, Ted Sims, on a blind date. The newlyweds moved to Tacoma, Wash., and bought a weekly newspaper, but sold it when Sims was recruited for his current position as chief engineer for Howard University's radio station.

In Washington, D.C., Perez spent eight years working on Capitol 9 Hill for prominent Washington Republicans—as a legislative aide and acting spokesperson for Sen. Slade Gorton, as press secretary for Congressman John Miller—and regional press secretary for the Bush '88 campaign at the Republican National Convention.

When she heard the new first lady was looking for a press secre- 10 tary, Perez did something that is never—never—done in official Washington: she asked for the job. And she asked a number of big-name politicians to ask on her behalf. "My mom always said the quickest way not to get what you want in the world is not to ask for it," she says of her unorthodox strategy.

Twenty years later, Perez is giving her own kids that same advice. 11 "One of the best things about this job is when my kids come to see mom at the office, they're wandering around the *White House*. That means they won't be intimidated by symbols of power. They will know—I mean really *know*—anything is possible and if there are limitations on their life, it will be those they place on themselves."

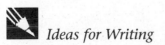 *A Second Look*

1 Randolph uses many facts and quotations to tell Anna Perez's story. How does she organize her material? Why does she begin as she does?

2 Stories like this one about the rise from poverty to prestige and power may sometimes sound like fairy tales. How does Randolph make her account realistic?

3 What does Perez mean when she says: "We were not defined by our financial situation. We were defined by our ability to overcome it" (paragraph 6)?

4 Perez says she wants her children to know that "anything is possible and if there are limitations on their life, it will be those they place on themselves." Do you agree with her view? Explain why or why not.

Ideas for Writing

Have you or someone you know overcome disadvantages to achieve success? (This should be success by your standards; it need not be equal to working in the White House.) Describe what this person did to attain success and how his or her attitude helped the advancement. In a brief essay, you cannot give a detailed account of every step toward success. Write down all you can think of; then go back and choose those that seem most important. The simplest way to arrange your material is chronologically, but you may wish to move back and forth between past and present as Laura Randolph does. If so, work carefully. This kind of writing needs clear transitions.

The Company Man

Ellen Goodman

Looking Forward

Phil, the subject of Ellen Goodman's essay, is a type frequently seen in many countries, but especially in modern America. He is a "company man": loyal to his employer, dedicated to his job, completely dependable, very hard working, no nonsense. He is, apparently, the perfect employee and an admirable man. But there is one other thing we should know. Goodman tells us in her opening sentence.

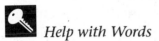 *Help with Words*

obituary *(paragraph 2):* published announcement of a death
coronary thrombosis *(paragraph 2):* heart attack
conceivably *(paragraph 3):* possibly
discreetly *(paragraph 16):* carefully, guardedly

H e worked himself to death, finally and precisely, at 3:00 1
A.M. Sunday morning.

The obituary didn't say that, of course. It said that he died of a 2
coronary thrombosis—I think that was it—but everyone among his
friends and acquaintances knew it instantly. He was a perfect Type
A, a workaholic, a classic, they said to each other and shook their
heads—and thought for five or ten minutes about the way they
lived.

This man who worked himself to death finally and precisely at 3
3:00 A.M. Sunday morning—on his day off—was fifty-one years old
and a vice-president. He was, however, one of six vice-presidents,

and one of three who might conceivably—if the president died or retired soon enough—have moved to the top spot. Phil knew that.

He worked six days a week, five of them until eight or nine at 4
night, during a time when his own company had begun the four-day week for everyone but the executives. He worked like the Important People. He had no outside "extracurricular interests," unless, of course, you think about a monthly golf game that way. To Phil, it was work. He always ate egg salad sandwiches at his desk. He was, of course, overweight, by 20 or 25 pounds. He thought it was okay, though, because he didn't smoke.

On Saturdays, Phil wore a sports jacket to the office instead of a 5
suit, because it was the weekend.

He had a lot of people working for him, maybe sixty, and most of 6
them liked him most of the time. Three of them will be seriously considered for his job. The obituary didn't mention that.

But it did list his "survivors" quite accurately. He is survived by 7
his wife, Helen, forty-eight years old, a good woman of no particular marketable skills, who worked in an office before marrying and mothering. She had, according to her daughter, given up trying to compete with his work years ago, when the children were small. A company friend said, "I know how much you will miss him." And she answered, "I already have."

"Missing him all these years," she must have given up part of 8
herself which had cared too much for the man. She would be "well taken care of."

His "dearly beloved" eldest of the "dearly beloved" children is a 9
hard-working executive in a manufacturing firm down South. In the day and a half before the funeral, he went around the neighborhood researching his father, asking the neighbors what he was like. They were embarrassed.

His second child is a girl, who is twenty-four and newly married. 10
She lives near her mother and they are close, but whenever she was alone with her father, in a car driving somewhere, they had nothing to say to each other.

The youngest is twenty, a boy, a high-school graduate who has 11
spent the last couple of years, like a lot of his friends, doing enough odd jobs to stay in grass and food. He was the one who tried to grab at his father, and tried to mean enough to him to keep the man at home. He was his father's favorite. Over the last two years, Phil stayed up nights worrying about the boy.

The boy once said, "My father and I only board here." 12

At the funeral, the sixty-year-old company president told the 13
forty-eight-year-old widow that the fifty-one-year-old deceased
had meant much to the company and would be missed and would
be hard to replace. The widow didn't look him in the eye. She was
afraid he would read her bitterness and, after all, she would need
him to straighten out the finances—the stock options and all that.

Phil was overweight and nervous and worked too hard. If he 14
wasn't at the office, he was worried about it. Phil was a Type A, a
heart-attack natural. You could have picked him out in a minute
from a lineup.

So when he finally worked himself to death, at precisely 3:00 A.M. 15
Sunday morning, no one was really surprised.

By 5:00 P.M. the afternoon of the funeral, the company president 16
had begun, discreetly of course, with care and taste, to make in-
quiries about his replacement. One of three men. He asked around:
"Who's been working the hardest?"

A Second Look

1 What specific details in Goodman's essay show that Phil was a good
"company man"?

2 What effects have Phil's work habits had on each of the other members
of his family? Be specific.

3 What is the company's attitude toward the death of its "man"?

4 Why does Goodman use the kinds of detail we find in paragraph 13?
What does she suggest about these people?

5 One of Goodman's major points—probably the most important one—is
never stated directly; it is implied or suggested by the whole essay.
What do you think it is?

Ideas for Writing

1 You may know a company man or company woman. If so, describe this
person. Tell your readers (who do not know your subject) about his or
her work habits, personal habits, family relationships, and so forth.
What do you think drives this person to be a workaholic?

2 Write an obituary for yourself, the kind you hope will appear when you
are gone—many years from now. Give the newspaper readers information about your age, work, religious or social affiliations, survivors,
whatever you want to be recorded and remembered.

Blue-Collar Journal:
A College President's Sabbatical

John R. Coleman

Looking Forward

In the spring of 1973, John R. Coleman—then President of Haverford College, a noted economist, and chair of the board of directors of the Federal Reserve Bank of Philadelphia—asked for and received a sabbatical, an academic leave with pay. He told few people of his plans. For eight weeks, President John Coleman became plain Jack Coleman, common laborer. Traveling about, Coleman was (among other things) a sewer-line construction worker, a dish washer, and a trash collector. During this time, he kept a journal of his activities. The following entry was made while Coleman was working as a salad man at the Union Oyster House in Boston.

 Help with Words

blitz *(paragraph 4):* a sudden, heavy military offensive
forage *(paragraph 13):* hunt or scavenge for food
respite *(paragraph 13):* rest, relief
fray *(paragraph 28):* battle

Sunday, March 18

I would feel cheated if I had lived out my life without experiencing a day like today. 1

Saturday's crowds or poor inventory policy or a combination of 2
the two left us short of almost everything today except for the

131

seafood itself. On Sunday there is no way to get new stocks. We must wait until the markets open on Monday morning.

In spite of radio warnings of snow, the dining rooms were packed 3 from 1:00 until 9:00. The first sign that we were in trouble came about 2:00. The early warning came from the cherry tomatoes. One of them goes in each of the tossed salads, and one of the tossed salads goes with almost every plate of food. The crisis atmosphere generated by the news that there were no more tomatoes so early in the day was startling. Shock on all sides. But that event was followed hard by the news that the cucumbers had also given out. A slice of them goes in each salad too.

Now it was like moving into blitz conditions in wartime. 4

"What are we supposed to do?" one of the waitresses moaned. 5 "Tossed salads always have a tomato and a piece of cucumber." I saw almost 150 years of Oyster House history being swept away in one evening.

"We'll just make do without them," another said. She was the 6 type who sang "There'll Always Be an England" in London's air-raid shelters in 1943.

"But we can't serve just plain lettuce," the first one sighed. 7

Fortunately, that possibility was soon removed. The cut salad 8 greens ran out about 4:00. We had had only four or five plastic bags of them to start the day, and that was nowhere near enough. Rationing the dwindling stock had failed dismally; no waitress was going to give her customers less than a full bowl of greens. But we still had a substitute: we could fall back on chopping up the two cases of whole lettuce that lay on the cooler's shelves.

I chopped up the heads and washed them as fast as I could, all the 9 while trying to keep up with the sandwich orders coming in.

"We're out of salad," each new waitress coming on duty called 10 out. That was like calling the civil defense office to alert them that the enemy was coming while the volunteers there were fighting a pitched battle in the headquarters yard itself.

"I know already," I called out from the cutting table in the back. 11

I cut not only the lettuce but my hand as well. Band-Aids didn't 12 stem the flow of blood as fast as I thought they would. I wondered when the first-aid corps would come by.

The last piece of the newly chopped lettuce went into the dining 13 room about 6:30. We then brought in reinforcements: the assistant manager went out to see what he could forage from other restaurants in the area. They were under attack too, and eight heads were all they could spare. That brought us half an hour of respite. I combed the garbage for some outer leaves that I had rejected earlier as being below the house standard. They were pressed into service now. I think I even washed them first.

Meanwhile, there was news of fresh disasters. The strawberry 14 shortcake gave out for a full two hours, until the chef was able to bake more. One waitress in that period managed to sell a customer a shortcake using cornbread as the base. I hoped someone would cite her later for exceptional service under fire.

The Boston cream pie ran out about 6:00. The whole wheat bread 15 and the rye went at about the same time. The stock of sour-cream cups and whipping cream had disappeared while I was chopping lettuce, and there was a long period before I got around to fixing more.

The dinner noise got louder. 16

"Two chicken club sandwiches, no mayonnaise on one." 17

"There's no butterscotch pudding here." 18

"Could you just slice one tomato for a customer who insists on 19 a salad?"

"Toast for Newburg." 20

"Give me a deluxe shrimp cocktail. But take your time—the old 21 goat can wait."

"I know you're busy, but can you open this fruit salad jar?" 22

"A lady says the crab tastes funny." 23

"Is there any more gingerbread?" 24

"Half a grapefruit." 25

"Where's my crabmeat salad? Who's the bitch that picked it up?" 26

One good thing was that, once we ran out of salad greens, no one 27 but me knew we were out of French dressing too.

And so it went all evening long. Surprisingly, no one suffered 28 much shock once that first terrible news about the cherry tomatoes had sunk in. It was chins up and into the fray from then on.

I had been wondering what the assistant manager does besides 29 look stern, unlock the lobster safe, and borrow lettuce. I found out in the midst of the panic that he was the one to whom I should report that the seat in the men's toilet had fallen off. (I forget how I had time to discover that casualty.)

It was a cold and clear night when I came out at 9:45. There was a 30 full moon over the plaza. The promised snow hadn't amounted to anything at all. But the square was empty just the same. We had met the enemy, and they had run.

A Second Look

1 Coleman gives an amusing and realistic picture of several fast-paced hours in the kitchen of the Union Oyster House. What are some of the techniques he uses to bring this scene to life for his readers?

2 Coleman describes the 1:00 to 9:00 shift as if it were a battle in which the action ebbs and flows. Pick out some of the words and phrases he uses to give this impression.

3 Why does Coleman say: "I would feel cheated if I had lived out my life without experiencing a day like today" (paragraph 1)?

4 When Coleman went to work at the Union Oyster House, he worried that friends or former students living in Boston might recognize him. In fact, none of the customers paid any attention to him. "At the college," he wrote in another entry, "I have become accustomed to being noticed when I walk into a room." But Jack Coleman the salad man went unrecognized: "Probably . . . my uniform is the best disguise I could have." What does this suggest about people and the jobs they hold?

Ideas for Writing

Describe an interesting day (or part of a day) at a job you have held. Show the reader what the job is *really* like. Describe the people with whom you are working. Tell how they interact. Use interesting details and active language so that the workplace comes alive for the reader, just as the kitchen of the Union Oyster House does.

As before, begin by listing everything you can think of about the job, the people, the particular day you are going to describe. Then go through this material, determining what is useful and what is not. You might arrange your essay chronologically. You should also consider focusing on the place where you work (how it is laid out) or on the people. Choose the pattern of organization you think will make your workday most interesting to your readers.

Out of Work in America

Roger Rosenblatt

Looking Forward

The severe recession that began in 1990 is only one of a series of economic downturns occurring over several decades. Each time the economy slips, many Americans lose their jobs. As Roger Rosenblatt points out, financial hardship is only part of what the unemployed suffer. Even worse, perhaps, is the loss of self-esteem.

 Help with Words

unctuous *(paragraph 1):* seemingly, but not actually, sincere and concerned (literally, oily or greasy)

incompetence *(paragraph 2):* inability, inadequacy

debacles *(paragraph 5):* terrible failures, downfalls

guinea *(paragraph 7):* a British gold coin (no longer in use)

exude *(paragraph 8):* send out, emit, radiate

inept *(paragraph 11):* awkward, unable to perform satisfactorily

chronically *(paragraph 11):* occurring for a long period of time

sedition *(paragraph 11):* disloyalty, treachery

expelled *(paragraph 13):* cast out

O nly once has the scene been portrayed realistically, and   1
that was in the movie *Broadcast News*. The news division
of the TV network in the movie is firing employees wholesale.
One man, who has worked there forever, is told by his unctuous
boss: "Now, if there's *anything* I can do for you." The ex-employee
responds with equal warmth: "Well, I certainly hope you *die*
soon."

He might have added, "slowly and with severe pain," but the   2
sentiments were implied. The fury at being fired not for incompetence but so that a company can cut costs is wild and deep.
Soon it turns on itself like a maddened animal. Eventually, if there is
no new job at hand, anger flattens out to a sense of helplessness,
then to rattling self-doubt, and finally takes the form of gazing into
space.

People all over America are running through such emotions   3
these days. Since the recession was declared official in July 1990, 1.4
million unemployed have been added to the rolls. In May the unemployment rate increased from 6.6 percent to 6.9 percent. The out-of-
work now total 8.6 million, which does not include 5.9 million who
work part-time but seek full-time jobs.

These people have become words in the news, the casualties   4
of "layoffs" and "cutbacks." Some are "involuntary part-timers."
All have been tossed out of the work that they know and that they
do best.

The companies that are doing the tossing are sometimes to blame,   5
sometimes not. A few places have been forced to decrease staffs
because of the junk bond and S&L debacles. Some others are belat-
edly paying penalties for overstaffing and thoughtless management. Most are simply corporate victims of hard times.

For the people who have been laid off, the results are the same: 6
They have become exiles in their own country, isolated from
friends, neighbors, their pasts, their senses of purpose and self—
cast out of America's history and future.

To be out of a job in America is like a special punishment of the   7
gods, two gods in particular: money and work. The feelings of

safety and social stature that come from having money are not pecu-
liarly American. Lord Byron once wrote a friend: "They say that
knowledge is power. I used to think so, but I now know that they
meant money. . . . Every guinea is a philosopher's stone. . . . Cash is
virtue." If one turns to the Bible for another, more spiritual view,
there's no help in Ecclesiastes: "Wine maketh merry: but money
answereth all things."

Work, however, is the national engine, the way America recog- 8
nizes itself. The sense of forcefulness that the country likes to exude
is connected to labor, and labor to character. One seeks "honest
work." The kid who gets a paper route or who splits rails and grows
up to be President embraces a national destiny 225 years old,
even older.

America, in the beginning, had to be made, and that took work. 9
Since every individual American is taught to be self-made, that too
takes work. You are a product of your own labors. You are what
you do.

When a man or a woman is deprived of work, then, the feeling of 10
isolation is overwhelming. Exile is sometimes a precondition for
clear-sightedness or superiority of vision, but not in the case of the
out-of-work in America. They may view their country more clearly,
but what they learn is how closely tied they have been to their country's nature and will. One moment they are swimming in the national current, the next they are strangers to themselves.

One reason, I think, that America has been so inept at helping the 11
chronically out-of-work is that there is a national resentment toward those who cannot hack it. It's not that Americans resist the
idea of welfare because they dread big government; given other con-
texts, such as social security, they adore big government. But they
see joblessness as a kind of crime or sin, an act of sedition. When
politicians speak of getting people off public assistance and back on
the job, it always sounds like a moral lecture. The lesson is: Idleness
is un-American.

I think of the man in *Broadcast News* as a real person, male or 12
female, and I wonder how he is doing. If he's lucky, he has a pension
after his long years of service or a nest egg somewhere. Even so, he
has been separated from his country and from himself by that news
division which, as if engaging in deliberate cruelty, sends him tele-

vised reports on how the economy continues to shrink, and how many more like him are made castaways.

Each new day opens to him full of bright and empty air. He has been expelled by the New World, and he searches for another. But there is no other. 13

 *A Second Look*

1 This essay is primarily an analysis of a situation and an expression of the writer's opinion. How does he support that opinion?

2 Overall, how does Rosenblatt organize the essay? List his major points. How does he move from one to another?

3 Rosenblatt says of those who have been laid off: "They have become exiles in their own country, isolated from friends, neighbors, their pasts, their senses of purpose and self—cast out of America's history and future" (paragraph 6). Explain why they feel this way.

4 According to the author, why has America done such a poor job of helping the long-term unemployed?

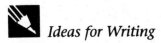 *Ideas for Writing*

Some say that Americans are particularly likely to judge others according to their work; in effect, they believe that "you are what you do." Do you believe that we tend to judge others in this way, or do we look more closely at the person than at the work he or she does? Write an essay expressing your opinion and giving specific examples to support it. If you can give examples from personal experience, that is particularly strong support.

Making Connections

Ellen Goodman and Roger Rosenblatt look at examples of the negative or destructive aspects of work. Laura B. Randolph and John R. Coleman see the positive side. How are the examples described by Randolph and Coleman different from those described by Goodman and Rosenblatt? Considering the people described in the four essays, what sort of general statement could you make about the varying attitudes toward work and self?

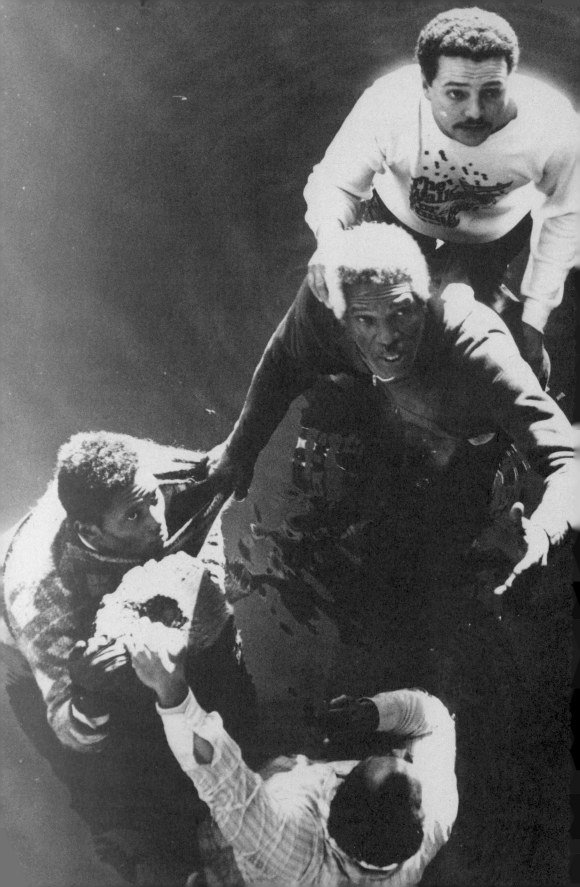

Heroism

Where Have All the Heroes Gone?

Pete Axthelm

Looking Forward

In this essay about heroism, Pete Axthelm not only identifies heroes from the past, he also considers whether our modern society is capable of producing twentieth-century heroes. He points out that most Americans are suspicious of courageous deeds and that the media are fast to expose any flaws of so-called heroes. Nevertheless, Americans still respect heroism and admire bravery and daring whenever they find true examples of it.

Help with Words

unabashed *(paragraph 2):* unashamed, unembarrassed
carping *(paragraph 2):* finding fault
martial *(paragraph 2):* warlike
alleged *(paragraph 2):* assumed but not proven
technocrats *(paragraph 2):* specialist in technology
scrutinize *(paragraph 3):* look closely at
barrage *(paragraph 3):* heavy artillery fire; here, a prolonged attack of words and accusations
bureaucrats *(paragraph 4):* officials who follow routine
legions *(paragraph 4):* large groups
prattle *(paragraph 4):* talk foolishly
elusive *(paragraph 5):* hard to define
chic *(paragraph 6):* fashionable

segment *(paragraph 6):* a part
artifacts *(paragraph 7):* man-made objects, especially very old ones
reputedly *(paragraph 7):* according to popular belief
stark *(paragraph 7):* extremely simple
idiom *(paragraph 11):* a style of speaking

Be Silent, Friend
Here Heroes Died
To Blaze a Trail
For Other Men

Near that sign at the door of the Alamo, there are several   1
simpler warnings. NO SMOKING. QUIET. GENTLEMEN RE-
MOVE HATS. I did not see anyone light up inside the Alamo. There
were few noises except for the subdued and reverent words of the
tour guides. The gentlemen were all bareheaded. And somehow
these minor gestures of respect seemed important. Standing in the
dusty courtyard in the dry Texas heat, in a season when Americans
were knifing one another over tanks of gasoline, I felt refreshed to
be in a place where the memory of heroism and trailblazing can still
make a friend take off his hat.

I have been reading quite a bit lately about how America has   2
grown too rich, too confused, or too sophisticated for heroes. John
Wayne is gone, his larger-than-life adventures replaced mainly by
movies that offer only blinding special effects or characters trying to
find themselves. Even when a rare film like "The Deer Hunter"
attempts to portray an unabashed war hero, nobody notices: The
critical reaction is mainly carping about its martial philosophy or
alleged racism. Sports stars, once expected to embody heroism as
well as talent, have lost much of their luster and our trust in a flurry
of team-hopping and renegotiation of contracts. The astronauts
have been smugly dismissed as technocrats, their heritage reduced
to a nervous summer of Skylab jokes. Once, we routinely asked our
kids who their heroes were. Today we fumble for answers when
they ask us if there are any heroes left.

Vietnam and Watergate played their part in all this, as we learned   3
to beware our leaders and to scrutinize them, warts and all. The
media have done so with a vengeance, and few leaders can stand up
to the barrage. But a cynical age now accepts the tarnished coin of
celebrity in place of heroic virtue—and thus the best-seller lists are
filled with books by Watergate felons and their co-conspirators.

Destiny: I am not convinced of the impossibility of modern hero-   4
ism. Anyone who has met the coal miners of eastern Kentucky or
the firemen of the South Bronx would be foolish to proclaim the
death of self-sacrifice or bravery—qualities that surely have some
relation to heroism. Can an era be hopelessly bleak and unheroic
when two young journalists can help to bring down a corrupt ad-
ministration and a few bureaucrats stand up to expose the waste
and carelessness of the bureaucracies that they serve? Even in a
troubled land of cookie-cutter shopping malls and thought-deaden-
ing discos, I suspect there are a few people who still seek out the
lonely roads, take the personal risks and dare to shape their world.
While modern legions may prattle about human potential, those
few actually fulfill it. And call it destiny.

Before trying to define or search for heroism, I wanted to reach   5
out and touch that elusive quality. Surely men touched it at Valley
Forge or San Juan Hill, on the Bad Lands of the frontier or the Sea of
Tranquility. But few felt it on more intimate terms than the Texas
freedom fighters of the 1830s. So the Alamo seemed as good a place
as any to make a start.

Some visitors have been disappointed by this small, modest   6
shrine in the midst of downtown San Antonio. Today, the Alamo
must battle for tourists' attention against the chic Riverwalk and
teeming streets nearby. On a corner a block away, for example, a
large sign over a servicemen's Christian center proclaims: RIGHT-
EOUSNESS EXALTETH A NATION. I did not see any servicemen in the
center as I passed. But at night, a segment of the city's large hooker
population works that corner. I asked one girl there about the Al
amo. "I'm from Miami, what do I know about that crap?" she said.
"You ain't another one of those John Wayne freaks, are you?" An
unpromising backdrop for history.

But the Alamo overcomes. In its resistance to the vast scale of   7
Texas, it asserts a stubborn grandeur of its own. Its artifacts are sim-
ple, its tone understated. In one display case is a rifle with which
Davy Crockett reputedly killed 350 bears in one summer. "That's

only a legend, of course," tour guide Lupe Nava warns softly. "But Crockett was such a good marksman that it could be true." The heroes, Crockett and Jim Bowie and commanding officer William Travis and the rest, are never oversold here. In merciful contrast to the stars of our modern tourist attractions, they are never depicted in life-size "multimedia presentations" that can only serve to cut the subjects down to size. Their story is stark, their memory vivid on its own terms. I think there are some lessons in this. . . .

An independent Republic of Texas was what the heroes of the   8 Alamo wanted. The price was their lives, and the odds against them were about 30 to 1. They knew the odds and played out the deadly game. But they fought so bravely that Santa Anna's huge Mexican Army was weakened. Forty-six days after the fall of the Alamo in 1836, another Texas army routed the Mexicans at San Jacinto. The Alamo had been remembered and avenged, and Texas was free. In death, the heroes of the Alamo had reshaped their world. In doing so, they had taken a fierce self-respect to the level of heroism—and provided a working definition that endures and illuminates.

Some comparisons are irresistible. Jim Bowie, among the oldest   9 Alamo fighters at forty-one, was a wealthy landowner with connections in high places. Today, when the lower classes do our fighting and wealth and connections smooth many a journey through politics or business, it may be hard to grasp the ideals that drove Bowie to the Texas war—and kept him there even after he was stricken with typhoid pneumonia. Bowie died, his famous knife bloodied, while fighting from his sickbed. . . .

James Butler Bonham was a courier who left the Alamo during   10 the siege and rode to Goliad, ninety-five miles away, to plead for reinforcement. He is less known than Crockett or Bowie, but his horse, it seems to me, should gallop through our modern consciousness. . . . The commander at Goliad could offer no troops. At that moment, Bonham knew that the Alamo was doomed. But he turned around, fought his way back through the Mexican Army and rejoined his comrades to fight to a certain death.

Challenge: No one faced the odds more squarely than Bonham.   11 No one had more options. Already a hero, he could have joined other Texas forces, fought to other glories, grabbed a few more days or years for a life that ended at twenty-nine. In the modern idiom that replaces self-respect with self-serving, he could have coped. It is difficult even to speculate on the depths of Bonham's dedication.

Perhaps modern analysts would speak of obsession, self-destructive tendencies, [or] male bonding among heroes. But the hoofbeats of Bonham's ride express it much better. They leave us with the lingering and essential challenge: Who among modern heroes would have made that return trip? . . .

Human Nature: On my way home from the Alamo, I stopped in 12 Nashville to talk with songwriter Tom T. Hall, whose country music salutes countless everyday heroes. "I think that heroism is basic to human nature," Hall said. "We look at Martin Luther King or the Pope going into Communist Poland, and we can't really avoid the possibilities of heroism. Maybe our own kind takes a much smaller form, like going into a mine shaft every morning or making the refrigerator payments in time to keep a family eating. But it's there. Given the chance, I think a lot of guys in mines or factories would make that ride back into the Alamo."

Those words may be hard to believe. But to stop believing them 13 would be like smoking in the Alamo. To deny modern heroism, it seems to me, is to admit that the odds are too long, the game no longer worth playing. Without heroes, we lose something of ourselves. I do not believe that we will ever accept that loss without listening one more time for hoofbeats.

A Second Look

1 What typical sources of heroism does Axthelm mention in paragraph 2? Why are these heroes no longer acceptable?

2 In what ways have the Vietnam War and the Watergate scandal influenced Americans' attitudes toward heroes?

3 Axthelm singles out James Butler Bonham for special notice. Why should Bonham be considered more courageous than the other fighters at the Alamo?

4 In explaining Bonham's options, Axthelm says, "he could have coped." What does the popular word *coped* mean in this sentence?

5 Why does Axthelm frequently mention the hoofbeats of Bonham's horse? (See paragraphs 10, 11, and 13.)

6 Review the characteristics of the Alamo fighters mentioned in paragraph 8, and then write the definition of *heroism* that this paragraph suggests.

Ideas for Writing

In groups assigned by your instructor, write down the names of as many modern heroes as you can think of. Give reasons for your choices. (Remember that Axthelm mentions self-sacrifice and bravery as heroic qualities.) Then select one of the names and write a paper in which you explain why you think this person is a modern hero. If you need to know more about the person you choose, you might check the library for further information. Your instructor or a librarian can suggest useful sources of material.

Forgotten

Peggy Say and Peter Knobler

Looking Forward

Terry A. Anderson, a correspondent for the Associated Press, was kidnapped in Beirut on March 16, 1985. At first, his family waited anxiously for the U.S. government to secure the release of Anderson and the other hostages; but after little happened, Peggy Say, Anderson's sister, decided she must do something on her own. For over five years, she worked for Anderson's freedom—talking to countless government officials, meeting with Presidents Reagan and Bush and former President Carter, making trips to the Middle East where she met with Yasser Arafat, and becoming a sort of unofficial spokesperson for the hostage families. In the following selection from her book, Say describes her emotional meeting with Brian Keenan, an Irish hostage released in August 1990.

Help with Words

deteriorated *(paragraph 1):* gotten worse

contended *(paragraph 6):* struggled, dealt with

elaborate *(paragraph 9):* add details

bizarre *(paragraph 13):* fantastic, weird

Islamic Jihad *(paragraph 21):* name of the group holding the hostages

priorities *(paragraph 27):* things ranked according to importance

introspective *(paragraph 28):* inward looking, reflective

dissipate *(paragraph 37):* scatter, vanish

atonement *(paragraph 37):* repentance, making up for a wrong

initiatives *(paragraph 41):* undertakings, projects

logistical *(paragraph 41):* referring to the movement of people or
     materials; here, referring to planning

David and Dad and Rich *(paragraph 44):* David is Peggy Say's
     husband. Dad is Glenn Richard Anderson, Sr., father of Say and
     Anderson, who died of cancer in February 1986. Rich is Glenn
     Richard Anderson, Jr., a brother. He died in June 1986, also of
     cancer.

O n August 24, Irish hostage Brian Keenan was released. I had very mixed feelings about going to Ireland to see him. It had been several years since I had had firsthand reports about Terry's life and conditions, and I wasn't at all sure that I wanted to hear about them now. What if things had deteriorated? What if Terry was sick or had been beaten or, worst of all, had lost all hope of freedom?

I knew that it had been almost a year since Brian had seen my brother, but, given the awful amount of time that had passed since Terry was taken, a year seemed like the recent past. I finally decided to stop being a baby about it and left for Ireland. After all, I had always insisted that if Terry could take it I could. . . .

By the time Brian and I collided in a bearhug in his hotel room, I was an emotional wreck. As he pulled back to look at me, Brian said laughingly, "Why, you even look like him!"

"All of us Andersons tend to look like one another as we grow older," I said, "which is not too bad for the men of our clan but isn't thrilling for the women."

Odd, but Brian Keenan reminded me of Terry. When he got up as we were talking and paced a little, he walked like Terry. Certain ways he'd turn his head, certain expressions he used, reminded me physically of Terry.

I started talking and couldn't stop. I just flat unloaded on this innocent victim. Poor Brian. He hadn't contended with enough in the past four and a half years, now he had me to deal with.

Words tumbled over one another and I didn't pause long enough between questions to allow him to answer.

"I'm so glad that you're out, and I know your sisters and all that they have done for you, and how difficult it has been and what a wonderful job they have done. How long has it been since you saw Terry?"

"Eleven months," he said. I didn't wait for him to elaborate, I just plowed on ahead.

"What does Terry know? How was he treated? How is his health? How is his mental health?"

Keenan hadn't seen Terry in almost a year but he said that the night before he was released he was taken into what he knew to be

Terry and Tom Sutherland's room. He felt they had been taken out of there only temporarily because all of their things were still there. He explored the room and found Terry's Bibles. Terry was doing a historical study of the Bible, he said, and had learned French, apparently from Tom Sutherland. He had a Bible in French as well as a Catholic and a Protestant Bible in English. Brian found a book of Tom's with a letter in it from Tom's wife that had been published in a Beirut paper.

Keenan said what particularly convinced him that it was their room was that Terry and Tom were the only two of the hostages who demanded to be clean-shaven and so had been furnished with shaving gear. There were two sets of shaving gear in the room.

There were two bolts on the wall that the hostages' eighteen-inch chains usually hung from. Pushed up next to the wall, close enough so Terry could ride it and still remain chained, was an exercise bicycle. That bizarre picture stayed in my mind. Terry in his underwear on his exercise bike. I could just kind of hear him clanking and pedaling, pedaling and clanking.

I kept asking Brian questions, and before he could really put the period to each sentence I was on to the next. "How long has it been? Who were you with? When were you moved? How were you treated?" I wanted to make so much noise that there would be no silence and I wouldn't have to ask the question, the one I had asked every single hostage, the second question after "Is Terry okay?" "Does Terry know what I'm doing and how does he feel about it?"

I have always been afraid, in the back of my mind, that I was not doing the right thing for Terry. What I was doing was obviously not having results; Terry was not out of there. Did this mean that I had done the wrong thing, that I had made the wrong choices? Would Terry blame me?

By the end I was trembling, shaking, and crying, and I just couldn't stop. I was not in control and I couldn't seem to get in control.

Brian was stunned. We sat almost knee to knee, and as I kept up this outburst he kind of retreated into his chair almost as if I were physically abusing him. Finally, when I was forced to gasp for breath, he interrupted me.

"Hold it! Just hold it! Get a grip on yourself, girl. This surely isn't what Terry needs when he gets out. He doesn't need a weeping, wailing woman to deal with. He needs the sister he left behind, the sister who stood so strong and dealt with the world on his behalf."

I snuffled myself into silence.   19

Brian assured me that Terry was aware of what I was doing . . .   20
and that he loved it. Terry had the best lines of communication of any of the hostages, he said, because of me: not only was Terry given the letters that we published in the Beirut papers on his birthdays, but every time there was a story about my travels or meetings the jailers showed it to him.

"Why," Brian laughed, "they told him one time they were going   21
to make you an honorary member of the Islamic Jihad. Terry said he didn't think you'd be too thrilled by that but thought they knew a fellow terrorist when they saw one."

There it was, the obvious opening for the dreaded question.   22
There was no avoiding it.

"Brian, if they liked or admired what I was doing, does that mean   23
that I prolonged Terry's captivity? Did they keep him so that I would continue to plead their cause?"

I didn't know that I wanted to hear his answer.   24

"Hell, no," he said. "Terry said that he knew the day he was taken   25
that it would be at least five years until he saw freedom again. He knew when Ben Weir was released that he'd be the last one out, and he's lived with that reality for the past five and a half years.

"Peggy, in captivity you learn to live with what is; not what you   26
want it to be, but what is. Terry has learned to live with his reality and he has no particular problem with that. What you've done is to provide him with a link to the outside world. Through your efforts he knows that he's not forgotten, that everyone has done their best to free him, and that one day, hopefully soon, he'll see freedom again."

The hostages were determined that the past was indeed the past,   27
he said. They had a life to get on with, and they wanted to put the past behind them. Their priorities had changed. They weren't out for revenge. . . .

For the hostages, the five and a half years had been like they'd   28
been for us, their families: cyclical. It's almost like the stages of grieving: first the denial, then the anger, finally the acceptance of what is. The hostages had passed through all those phases, and in the last year or two they had become very introspective, very moral.

They had made a pact with one another, Brian told me: they would do things with their lives on the outside that would have value, that would be moral, that would in their own ways make a better world. And each would see to it that the promises made in captivity were kept. If anybody started straying off the straight and narrow, the others would phone up and say, "Hey, get back on line here."

Terry wasn't angry? That made me angry.   29

"Sure," I told Keenan, "you guys have gone all holy and we've   30
become a bunch of hooligans."

I had kept a fantasy close to my heart. I had pictured myself tak- 31
ing Terry around to all the people who had turned their backs on me, everyone who had been callous or mean. I kept thinking, "All you people who hurt me, you just wait till my brother gets home. Are you going to be sorry." I had fed on this fantasy. I was going to make somebody accountable. I was going to make people look at Terry, and he would face down the ones who said they did nothing because publicity was going to prolong his captivity.

It wasn't going to be. I was not going to get my revenge, as little   32
and as unsatisfactory as it might have been. I had to accept that it wasn't going to happen. "Look, Peggy," Brian said, "there's nothing more you can do. Quit."

I was crying, just blubbering and shaking as I said to him, "Brian,   33
I don't know how. I don't know how to stop what I'm doing. I don't know anybody I can go to who can reassure me that 'Yes, you've done everything you can, it's going to be over with. Go home.'"

Brian said, "I'm telling you this, Peggy: you go home, and you'd   34
better get yourself in shape so that you can be there for Terry when he gets out. If he sees what I'm seeing now, he's not going to be able to deal with it."

I had so much churning inside of me that again I reacted physi- 35
cally. A few days after I returned from Ireland to Kentucky I was back in the hospital for my ulcers.

The downside was that I was in the hospital again. The upside   36
was that I was in complete isolation and I was finally able to reach some conclusions about these years.

Facing the fact of Terry's acceptance, his lack of anger, I felt mine   37
starting to dissipate, almost a physical release at the anger leaving me. I had always known it was not a pretty emotion: the desire for revenge, the desire for atonement, the desire to make somebody pay.

\

And as I began to heal emotionally I began to heal physically.   38

I realized I can't do any more than my part. I've had a role to play   39
in this, and the very fact that we sustained an unpopular issue for
five and a half years—that those who know there are hostages in
Lebanon know Terry Anderson, that I've given him a future—has
to be enough.

I thought about it for a long time afterward, and finally I realized   40
that my judgment of what I had done no longer depended on
Terry's opinion. If Terry were to come to me tomorrow and say,
"You did the wrong thing for me, you cost me an extra four and a
half years," or if he were to tell me that what I did was not helpful,
or that it was harmful, I finally feel secure enough that I could say to
him, "Well, Terry, I'm sorry to hear you feel that way but I did what I
felt I had to do." I'd feel bad about it, of course, but if I had it to do
over again I couldn't do it any other way.

Sure, all of us might have used different strategies, maybe dif-   41
ferent political initiatives; maybe we would have done some logistical things differently. But the morality of what I did was right. To
ignore what was happening would have been obscene. I could
never have lived with it. I could never have walked into the future,
as I am doing now, feeling whole and secure and right about what
I did.

And I know now, finally, that I don't have to look for my worth   42
in my brother's eyes, or anybody else's. I have to look for it in
my heart.

I did the only thing that I could do. Whether it was right or   43
wrong, whether it did or did not prolong Terry's captivity, I couldn't
not do it.

My fantasy of Terry's release has changed over the years. In the   44
beginning I pictured David and Dad and Rich and me, and we'd be
over in Wiesbaden, celebrating. Then it was going to be Rich and
David and me, then David and me. Little by little my fantasy
evaporated.

Terry's release is not going to be a time of joyous celebration. It   45
will be wonderful because Terry will have reached freedom, but
then I'm going to have to tell him about Dad and Rich, and help him
try to deal with the fact that his world, as it existed when he was
taken, is no longer there. And that's going to be difficult. But, after
all these years, I finally know I'm up to it.

AFTERWORD

Terry Anderson was freed on December 4, 1991, and reunited with his family the next day. He had been in captivity for over five and a half years—exactly 2,454 days. Asked what she would do now that her brother was finally free, Peggy Say responded that she looked forward to becoming herself again and not always being known as Terry Anderson's sister. Anderson, asked about being the longest-held hostage, said: "It's an honor I'd have gladly given up long ago." Terry Anderson, like the other freed hostages, is trying to reestablish a normal life and learn to deal with the effects of long captivity.

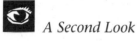 *A Second Look*

1 According to Brian Keenan, how did the hostages learn to endure their dreadful, sometimes terrifying, circumstances?

2 Why does Peggy Say begin to doubt that her activities on her brother's behalf are really helping him? Why does she finally decide that it does not matter whether they helped or not?

3 When Brian Keenan and several other hostages were released, they were welcomed home as heroes. Do you feel that Peggy Say and the other members of hostage families who worked with her also qualify as heroes? Explain your answers.

4 Some people, even though they were joyful when the hostages were released, have argued that these men and women were victims rather than heroes. Which would you call them? Explain your answer.

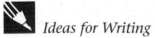 *Ideas for Writing*

Peggy Say was determined to help her brother, but she sometimes doubted that she was going about it the right way. Have you ever tried to accomplish something that you were certain was right but wondered if your methods were wrong? Describe this experience. You must explain carefully to your readers what you were trying to accomplish and how you went about it. Just as important, you must make the reader understand why you had feelings of doubt.

I Know Why the Caged Bird Sings

Maya Angelou

Looking Forward

Maya Angelou has established a wide reputation as a singer and actress as well as a writer. In this chapter from her autobiography, Angelou recalls the suspense and excitement in a small town in Arkansas over Joe Louis's match to keep the title of world heavyweight champion. Notice the ways in which Angelou shows the reader the importance of the match before she states this main idea directly.

 Help with Words

apprehensive *(paragraph 2):* fearful
cracker *(paragraph 3):* slang for a white person
assent *(paragraph 10):* approval
"master's voice" *(paragraph 12):* part of an advertising slogan for RCA
 radios and phonographs
maimed *(paragraph 16):* wounded or crippled
accusations *(paragraph 17):* charges
ordained *(paragraph 17):* divinely ordered
hewers *(paragraph 17):* cutters
ambrosia *(paragraph 27):* food for the gods
white lightning *(paragraph 27):* moonshine, homemade whiskey

he last inch of space was filled, yet people continued to 1
wedge themselves along the walls of the Store. Uncle Willie

had turned the radio up to its last notch so that youngsters on the porch wouldn't miss a word. Women sat on kitchen chairs, dining room chairs, stools and upturned wooden boxes. Small children and babies perched on every lap available and men leaned on the shelves or each other.

The apprehensive mood was shot through with shafts of gaiety, as a black sky is streaked with lightning.

"I ain't worried 'bout this fight. Joe's gonna whip that cracker like it's open season."

"He gone whip him till that white boy call him Momma."

At last the talking was finished and the string-along songs about razor blades were over and the fight began.

"A quick jab to the head." In the Store the crowd grunted. "A left to the head and a right and another left." One of the listeners cackled like a hen and was quieted.

"They're in a clench, Louis is trying to fight his way out."

Some bitter comedian on the porch said, "That white man don't mind hugging that niggah now, I betcha."

"The referee is moving in to break them up, but Louis finally pushed the contender away and it's an uppercut to the chin. The contender is hanging on, now he's backing away. Louis catches him with a short left to the jaw."

A tide of murmuring assent poured out the doors and into the yard.

"Another left and another left. Louis is saving that mighty right. . . ." The mutter in the Store had grown into a baby roar and it was pierced by the clang of a bell and the announcer's "That's the bell for round three, ladies and gentlemen."

As I pushed my way into the Store I wondered if the announcer gave any thought to the fact that he was addressing as "ladies and gentlemen" all the Negroes around the world who sat sweating and praying, glued to their "master's voice."

There were only a few calls for RC Colas, Dr. Peppers, and Hire's root beer. The real festivities would begin after the fight. Then even the old Christian ladies who taught their children and tried themselves to practice turning the other cheek would buy soft drinks, and if the Brown Bomber's victory was a particularly bloody one they would order peanut patties and Baby Ruths also.

Bailey and I lay the coins on top of the cash register. Uncle Willie didn't allow us to ring up sales during a fight. It was too noisy and might shake up the atmosphere. When the gong rang for the next round we pushed through the near-sacred quiet to the herd of children outside.

"He's got Louis against the ropes and now it's a left to the body 15 and a right to the ribs. Another right to the body, it looks like it was low. . . . Yes, ladies and gentlemen, the referee is signaling, but the contender keeps raining the blows on Louis. It's another to the body, and it looks like Louis is going down."

My race groaned. It was our people falling. It was another lynch- 16 ing, yet another Black man hanging on a tree. One more woman ambushed and raped. A Black boy whipped and maimed. It was hounds on the trail of a man running through slimy swamps. It was a white woman slapping her maid for being forgetful.

The men in the Store stood away from the walls and at attention. 17 Women greedily clutched the babes on their laps while on the porch the shufflings and smiles, flirtings and pinching of a few minutes before were gone. This might be the end of the world. If Joe lost we were back in slavery and beyond help. It would all be true, the accusations that we were lower types of human beings. Only a little higher than the apes. True that we were stupid and ugly and lazy and dirty and, unlucky and worst of all, that God Himself hated us and ordained us to be hewers of wood and drawers of water, forever and ever, world without end.

We didn't breathe. We didn't hope. We waited. 18

"He's off the ropes, ladies and gentlemen. He's moving towards 19 the center of the ring." There was no time to be relieved. The worst might still happen.

"And now it looks like Joe is mad. He's caught Carnera with a left 20 hook to the head and a right to the head. It's a left jab to the body and another left to the head. There's a left cross and a right to the head. The contender's right eye is bleeding and he can't seem to keep his block up. Louis is penetrating every block. The referee is moving in, but Louis sends a left to the body and it's the uppercut to the chin and the contender is dropping. He's on the canvas, ladies and gentlemen."

Babies slid to the floor as women stood up and men leaned to- 21 ward the radio.

"Here's the referee. He's counting. One, two, three, four, five, six, 22 seven . . . Is the contender trying to get up again?"

All the men in the Store shouted, "NO." 23

"—eight, nine, ten." There were a few sounds from the audience, 24
but they seemed to be holding themselves in against tremendous
pressure.

"The fight is all over, ladies and gentlemen. Let's get the micro- 25
phone over to the referee. . . . Here he is. He's got the Brown
Bomber's hand, he's holding it up. . . . Here he is. . . ."

Then the voice, husky and familiar, came to wash over us— 26
"The winnah, and still heavyweight champeen of the world . . .
Joe Louis."

Champion of the world. A Black boy. Some Black mother's son. 27
He was the strongest man in the world. People drank Coca-Colas
like ambrosia and ate candy bars like Christmas. Some of the men
went behind the Store and poured white lightning in their soft-
drink bottles, and a few of the bigger boys followed them. Those
who were not chased away came back blowing their breath in front
of themselves like proud smokers.

It would take an hour or more before the people would leave the 28
Store and head for home. Those who lived too far had made ar-
rangements to stay in town. It wouldn't do for a Black man and his
family to be caught on a lonely country road on a night when Joe
Louis had proved that we were the strongest people in the world.

A Second Look

1 Sometimes a writer deliberately exaggerates or overstates in order to
   make a point. Find several examples of such exaggeration in Angelou's
   narrative.

2 Why is Louis's victory so important to the listeners in the country store?

3 When we expect characters to behave in a certain way, but their behavior turns out to be the opposite of what we expect, that is one kind of
   irony. Explain the irony in paragraphs 13 and 28.

Ideas for Writing

1 Choose one of the following statements:

"Even though they play for fame and money, professional athletes can be real heroes."

"Professional athletes are in sports for the fame and money; they should not be considered real heroes."

Use the statement you choose as the main idea in an essay. Support your opinion with examples of sports figures you feel are or are not heroic. Remember that you must make your idea of "hero" clear before you can show that professional athletes do or do not qualify. Assume that your readers have not yet made up their minds on this issue. You must convince them.

2 Write a paragraph or two in which you describe the tension and excitement of the crowd just before a sports event begins. The writing will be much easier if you have a specific event in mind and let the reader know what it is. Here is a sample topic sentence: "Just before the tip-off of the city basketball championship game, energy surged through the crowd like electricity."

Stride Toward Freedom

Martin Luther King, Jr.

Looking Forward

In these paragraphs, Martin Luther King, Jr., who was himself a hero and probably the greatest leader in the history of the American civil rights movement, describes a simple action that many people saw as an act of heroism—a black woman refusing to give up her seat to a white man on a Montgomery bus. At the same time, Reverend King is explaining why something happened because this action marked the beginning of the famous Montgomery bus boycott. For days, the blacks of Montgomery, Alabama, refused to ride the public buses, leaving them nearly empty. This became a turning point in the civil rights movement, but its beginning was a single, brave act.

 Help with Words

accommodate *(paragraph 1):* make room for
speculation *(paragraph 2):* an opinion formed without enough evidence
plausible *(paragraph 2):* believable
persistent *(paragraph 2):* occurring again and again
invariable *(paragraph 2):* unchanging
unwarranted *(paragraph 3):* without foundation, undeserved
intrepid *(paragraph 3):* fearless
affirmation *(paragraph 3):* a strong positive statement
accumulated *(paragraph 3):* piled up
indignities *(paragraph 3):* disgraces, humiliations
aspirations *(paragraph 3):* desires, ambitions
impeccable *(paragraph 4):* without fault

On December 1, 1955, an attractive Negro seamstress, Mrs. 1
Rosa Parks, boarded the Cleveland Avenue bus in downtown Montgomery. She was returning home after her regular day's
work in the Montgomery Fair—a leading department store. Tired
from long hours on her feet, Mrs. Parks sat down in the first seat
behind the section reserved for whites. Not long after she took her
seat, the bus operator ordered her, along with three other Negro
passengers, to move back in order to accommodate boarding white
passengers. By this time every seat in the bus was taken. This meant
that if Mrs. Parks followed the driver's command she would have
to stand while a white male passenger, who had just boarded the
bus, would sit. The other three Negro passengers immediately com-
plied with the driver's request. But Mrs. Parks quietly refused. The
result was her arrest.

There was to be much speculation about why Mrs. Parks did not 2
obey the driver. Many people in the white community argued that
she had been "planted" by the NAACP in order to lay the groundwork for a test case, and at first glance that explanation seemed
plausible, since she was a former secretary of the local branch of the
NAACP. So persistent and persuasive was this argument that it convinced many reporters from all over the country. Later on, when I
was having press conferences three times a week—in order to accommodate the reporters and journalists who came to Montgomery
from all over the world—the invariable first question was: "Did the
NAACP start the bus boycott?"

But the accusation was totally unwarranted, as the testimony of 3
both Mrs. Parks and the officials of the NAACP revealed. Actually,
no one can understand the action of Mrs. Parks unless he realizes
that eventually the cup of endurance runs over, and the human personality cries out, "I can take it no longer." Mrs. Parks's refusal to
move back was her intrepid affirmation that she had had enough. It
was an individual expression of a timeless longing for human dignity and freedom. She was not "planted" there by the NAACP, or
any other organization; she was planted there by her personal sense
of dignity and self-respect. She was anchored to that seat by the
accumulated indignities of days gone by and the boundless aspirations of generations yet unborn. She was a victim of both the forces

of history and the forces of destiny. She had been tracked down by the Zeitgeist—the spirit of the time.

Fortunately, Mrs. Parks was ideal for the role assigned to her by 4 history. She was a charming person with a radiant personality, soft spoken and calm in all situations. Her character was impeccable and her dedication deep-rooted. All of these traits together made her one of the most respected people in the Negro community.

AFTERWORD

Rosa Parks, now in her late 70s, lives in Detroit where she spends many hours at the Rosa and Raymond Parks Institute for Self Development, an organization that works primarily with children. In a recent interview with Marie Ragghianti, Mrs. Parks said about the famous bus incident of 1955: "I had had enough. I wanted to be treated like a human being." One of the teenage girls that Rosa Parks has worked with at the Institute says of her: "Mrs. Parks doesn't think of herself as a heroine. She did it because it was right. She doesn't see herself as the Mother of the Civil Rights movement, but *I* see her as that. All children do." ("I Wanted to Be Treated Like a Human Being," *Parade*, January 19, 1992)

 A Second Look

1 King's essay (of which this is the beginning) shows cause and effect: Mrs. Parks's arrest was a cause; the bus boycott was the effect. He also shows cause-and-effect relationships in paragraphs 1 and 3. What are they?

2 Near the end of paragraph 3, King emphasizes the importance of his point by attracting our attention with repetition. Find several examples. Would even more repetition be effective? Why or why not?

3 In paragraph 1, King tells us a good deal about Mrs. Parks, mentioning her appearance, occupation, place of employment, and so forth. Since it is her action that becomes important, why does King give so much personal information about her? Is this a successful writing technique?

4 Moving from a bus seat may seem a small matter. Why did Mrs. Parks choose to go to jail rather than leave her seat?

5 In paragraph 3, King says that Mrs. Parks was "tracked down by . . . the spirit of the time." Why was the time right for an action such as hers?

Ideas for Writing

1 Sometimes a personal event such as Mrs. Parks's refusal to move or Joe Louis's fight can take on importance for large groups of people. The same is true for events involving relatively small groups of people, such as the Chinese students in Tiananmen Square or the freedom fighters in the Baltic capitals. In small groups or as a class, discuss recent examples. You might include anything from an environmental protest to an Olympic victory to a regional basketball championship. The only condition is that the events you name must have taken on importance for a larger group beyond the individuals or small groups involved, making those persons heroic.

   Choose one of these events as the subject of an essay. When you write, first describe the event for readers who may not be familiar with it. Tell about the person or persons involved. Explain clearly what they did. Then go on to show your readers why this event was important to others and why those you are writing about are heroes.

2 Complete the following sentence: "I would rather go to jail than ___." Then write a paragraph using this statement as the topic sentence and explaining why you feel so strongly about your subject.

Straight Talk About Heroes

Kathy M. Ponder

Looking Forward

Student writer Kathy M. Ponder presents her standards for heroism and finds that some whom the mass media call heroes meet these standards, whereas others do not. As you read, decide whether you agree with Ponder on the definition of *hero* and who should be given that label. This article appeared as a letter to the editor in a metropolitan newspaper.

 Help with Words

constitutes *(paragraph 1):* makes up
exceptional *(paragraph 2):* outstanding or superior
speculated *(paragraph 2):* guessed, thought to be true
mandatory *(paragraph 4):* compulsory, not optional

W hat makes a hero? Magic Johnson or Kimberly Bergalis? 1 First, we must know what constitutes a hero and who Johnson and Bergalis are. A hero is one noted for his courage, strengths, special achievements and daring acts (especially to risk or sacrifice one's life for others).

Johnson is a professional basketball player with exceptional play- 2 ing ability who tested HIV positive. It has been speculated that he contracted the virus through sexual promiscuity. Yet, the media dub him a hero.

By this, are we (as a nation) telling our children it is OK to be   3
sexually promiscuous or, if you are famous, you can still be considered a hero regardless of your actions? I do not consider Johnson a hero although I do admire the fact that he is now taking a stand on the AIDS issue.

On the other hand, Bergalis was an outstanding, highly moral   4
young lady who became infected with AIDS during a routine visit to her dentist—the first noted case of its kind. She did not engage in sexual relationships, use drugs, or participate in any other high-risk behavior. Her life might have been spared if there had been a mandatory law requiring health care professionals to inform their patients if they tested HIV positive.

In an effort to get legislation passed so that others would not have   5
to suffer as she did, Bergalis spoke before Congress. Although she is gone, she is a hero.

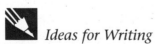 *A Second Look*

1   Look at Ponder's criteria for a hero in paragraph 1. Why does she believe that Bergalis meets these standards whereas Johnson does not? What might qualify Johnson as "semihero"?

2   Ponder says that Bergalis can be considered heroic in part because of her character: She was "an outstanding, highly moral young lady." Do you think heroism is related to character and morality?

3   This is a persuasive essay: Its purpose is to state an opinion and convince others of the worth of that opinion. Is the writer successful? Why or why not? Do you have any suggestions for revision?

Ideas for Writing

Write a letter to the editor of a city newspaper on any subject about which you feel strongly. You are stating your own opinion, one that you hold firmly, but there is no guarantee that your readers will agree with you. To persuade others, you need to explain your ideas clearly and support them as strongly as you can. Be sure that terms are carefully defined (like *hero* in paragraph 1 of Ponder's letter) and that important circumstances are clearly described.

Making Connections

At one point, Pete Axthelm says of the Alamo heroes that they "reshaped their world" and in the process provided a working definition of heroism by which we still measure heroes (paragraph 8). Kathy M. Ponder offers a somewhat different definition (paragraph 1), but daring and sacrifice are again involved. In small groups or as a class, try to construct a definition of *hero* that will cover all the persons your group considers heroic. (You may want to review the discussion for the writing assignment on page 148.)

Women and Men

Yes, Women and Men Can Be "Just Friends"

Marjorie Franco

Looking Forward

In this essay, Marjorie Franco begins with examples from her youth and builds up to the main idea, which is stated in paragraph 5. She shows by the arrangement of her ideas that men and women must first establish their own identities before they can form real friendships.

Help with Words

platonic *(paragraph 3):* free from sexual desire
mutual *(paragraph 4):* common or shared
astounded *(paragraph 4):* shocked or amazed
psychotherapist *(paragraph 5):* one who treats psychological disorders
siblings *(paragraph 5):* brothers and sisters
discomfiting *(paragraph 6):* confusing

I remember a summer day when I was ten years old: I was walking my dog, Lucky, in the South Side Chicago neighborhood where I grew up. Lucky strained at his leash, sniffing the trunk of the neighborhood's favorite climbing tree. Suddenly a wild shout startled me: "Look out, Rehn Peterson's sister!" and I saw Teddy Wilson, my brother's friend, on his Silver King bicycle, bearing down on me at top speed. With great presence of mind I leaped aside and, to Lucky's astonishment, slammed hard against the tree.

173

I was furious—not because I'd been very nearly run down by a bike, and not because I'd had the wind knocked out of me by a tree. I was outraged because Teddy Wilson had denied me my identity.

On that day something stirred in me. Until then I had given little thought to who I was. My brother, two years older, was close to me; I was his friend and I knew it. He had other friends, of course, boys—they were always around—and because I was my brother's friend I had assumed I was their friend, too. But on that summer day, in the eyes of Teddy Wilson, I was "Rehn Peterson's sister" and nothing more.

But I wanted more. And in the years that followed, because of that drive for identity, I gained some practical experience in platonic friendship. Never mind that my girlfriend Florence, who read *True Story*, had whispered hotly into my ear, "Boys have uncontrollable passions, and they can't help it." I hadn't noticed any uncontrollable passion, unless you want to count the time Teddy Wilson said I looked fat in my bathing suit, and in that case the uncontrollable passion was mine.

I became friends with my brother's boyfriends and remained so until we all grew up and scattered from the neighborhood. As a friend, I went with Roy to his senior prom because his girlfriend was out of town; I went to plays with Elmer because we had developed a mutual interest in the theatre; I learned to cook with Jack since we both liked to cook (we experimented in our parents' kitchens and astounded each other with unusual creations). And eventually I went for long walks with Teddy Wilson during which we told each other our troubles.

My early experiences laid the groundwork for the attitudes I carried into adult life. In a recent discussion with David M. Moss, Ph.D., psychotherapist on the staff of Lutheran General Hospital's Consultation Center in Park Ridge, Illinois, he told me, "The development of healthy friendships grows out of the trust we learn and experience in childhood. Self-trust and trust of others are learned as early as the first year in life. From then on the presence or absence of trust is relearned and reexperienced in relationships with siblings, peers, and authority figures." I learned from my experience that it is not only possible but also desirable and highly rewarding for women and men to have platonic friendships. Shared interests between a man and woman need not include sex.

"The richness of platonic relationships can be enjoyed," says Dr. 6
Moss, "if we draw responsible boundaries in our use of sexuality."
However, choosing to have platonic friendships does not necessarily correspond to what may be in the minds of others. Pressures
from outside a relationship can be very discomfiting.

Is it worth it, then? That depends. It's easier to be what others 7
expect us to be. It would have been easy for me to remain Rehn
Peterson's sister and let it go at that. Claiming identity is an effort.
But the effort has given me the pleasures of friendship and good
memories I will always keep.

A Second Look

1 According to the author, how is a strong self-identity related to platonic
   friendship?

2 It is possible to define a term without ever using a dictionary definition.
   What is Franco's method of defining platonic friendships in paragraph
   5? It is also possible to define by giving examples. What examples of
   platonic friendships does the author mention?

3 Why does Franco begin the essay with a personal experience? Point out
   some of the specific details that make the description of the experience
   interesting.

Ideas for Writing

1 Write about a relationship with someone you consider a platonic friend.
   Begin by choosing the person; then list the interests you have in common. Recall some specific experiences that show these common interests, and arrange them from earliest to most recent or from least to most
   important. When you write about this relationship, assume that your
   readers know what a platonic friendship is but that they have never met
   the friend you are describing.

2 Have you ever been treated like someone's son, daughter, brother, sister, or friend rather than as an individual? Describe that experience.
   Remember to use specific details.

Skiing with the Guys

Catherine Ettlinger

Looking Forward

When Catherine Ettlinger, former managing editor of *Mademoiselle* magazine, went heli-skiing with a group of advanced skiers, she found herself the only woman in the company of eleven men, "a macho bunch." In this article, she describes how she was able to become "one of the guys" and keep her feminine identity at the same time.

 Help with Words

careened *(paragraph 1):* tilted

pangs *(paragraph 2):* pains

pervasive *(paragraph 4):* widespread

relishing *(paragraph 6):* greatly enjoying

tabloid *(paragraph 6):* a newspaper often featuring sensational stories and headlines

non sequitur *(paragraph 8):* something that does not follow logically

preamble *(paragraph 8):* introductory remarks

veritable *(paragraph 9):* actual

litany *(paragraph 16):* series

epiphany *(paragraph 17):* a sudden revelation

maliciously *(paragraph 17):* cruelly or viciously

prowess *(paragraph 18):* ability

precariously *(paragraph 23):* dangerously

precluded *(paragraph 24):* prevented

traverses *(paragraph 25):* cross-overs

rendered *(paragraph 28):* made

pariah *(paragraph 28):* a misfit or outcast

The helicopter careened, climbed, dove, floated and hovered   1
until a safe landing was found: the point of a peak that
dropped sharply on all four sides, a vertical view down a mountainside in the Canadian Rockies that fell into the sky.

We stayed close to put on our skis, and then, following our guide,   2
Ian, one by one so as not to loosen the snow and start a slide, we
edged around the shoulder of the peak until we came to the mouth
of a wide gully that dropped at a 40-degree angle, one of the steep-
est pitches I'd ever seen. Just me and 11 guys, strangers in pursuit of
the ultimate ski experience. And though I'd done this before (this
was my third trip heli-skiing with Canadian Mountain Holidays in
the boonies of British Columbia), can-I-keep-up pangs were now
gathering in my gut.

Two of the guys started down after Ian, then two more, making   3
tracks that slithered away like snakes in the thigh-high April powder. The six others looked to me. This would be my reckoning. I
pushed off the lip, catching air (always good for points) and sank
into the champagne powder. As I rose to make my first turn I had
my rhythm: two, three, four turns, free-falling down the steep from
one to another, face shot after face shot of powder dusting my
glasses. After two dozen or so turns, the pitch flattened and my
tight turns became lovely, long loopy ones. Easing from edge to
edge and back again, I pulled up to the others, thinking this was
the absolute best that skiing has to offer. Endless expanses of
virgin wilderness in every direction. I felt like one of the luckiest
people alive.

It wasn't easy being a girl among guys out for a pure jock experi-   4
ence. Pervasive in the lodge is a locker-room logic that turns ava-
lanche scares and close-call falls into badges of courage—and any
woman into a stereotype who associates powder more with
makeup than skiing and who never goes anywhere her blow-dryer
can't go.

It had taken me two days to get into this group. I was put at first   5
with those who had come for the "Learn to Ski Powder Week"; no
questions asked, it went without saying that I couldn't keep up with
the big boys. But I was bored until I was moved up to the intermedi-

ate level in the afternoon. The next day I was promoted to the advanced group—a macho bunch—and skied with them until high winds forced us back to the lodge just before lunch the next day (the lodges are so isolated, they can be reached only by helicopter in the winter).

Deciding not to waste the afternoon indoors, I put on cross-coun- 6 try skis and took off along an old logging road, relishing the majesty of the mountains and the solitude. About an hour out I saw some cat tracks (as in cougar), and the city side of me did an about-face. I headed home to the lodge, visions of gruesome tabloid headlines dancing in my mind. Going along at a pretty good clip I ran into two guys headings out.

"Beautiful, isn't it?" I asked. 7

"Great exercise" was one guy's retort—a non sequitur, I thought. 8 That night after dinner the same guy, Reb (yes, that's short for Rebel—he'd already won points for wearing a T-shirt and shell when everyone else was bundled up in down), sat next to me and, without any preamble, asked, "Why aren't you married?" I asked why he was, and left for the far side of the room.

I'd encountered the same sort of boldness on my second heli-ski 9 trip: Early in the week three men, veritable strangers, had asked me to spend the night with them. At the time I was insulted. In retrospect I realized the offers were merely an extension of the macho flexing that underscores the whole heli-ski experience—and puts me, as a woman, on the outside.

Imagine how I felt, then, when the next morning at breakfast Reb 10 turned up again: "We had a deserter in our group; a guy was called back home for some emergency. Wanna join up?"

Like the army? "Is this a joke?" I asked. His was the fastest group 11 of the four.

"Nope. We want a woman." 12

"Filling a quota?" 13

"No, seriously, we heard you're a real good skier, and we'd like it 14 very much if you'd join us."

In that case (skier first, woman second): "Sure." 15

As my new group waited for the helicopter to pick us up in front 16 of the lodge, Dave, a third-year law student, began a litany of the dirtiest dirty jokes I'd ever heard. Was this for my benefit, to make me feel uncomfortable? The sinking feeling in the pit of my stomach returned. After we landed the jokes started all over again. Then Howard, a friend of Reb's and one of his three ski buddies from California, stepped to the edge of the ledge to urinate. Ian, our guide that day (the four guides rotate from group to group), warned, "Howard, watch it, you're getting kind of close." We all looked over, worried. Ian added: "Howard, you don't have much to hang on to out there." I was the first to laugh. . . .

Suddenly everything was different: I was one of the guys. I could   17
ski, and I could join in the fun too. Then and there I had an epiphany of sorts: Those dirty jokes weren't maliciously intended to make me feel uneasy and unwanted; they were simply part of the experience. Had they not told those jokes on my account, that would indeed have made me an outsider.

A funny thing happened after I joined the fraternity: My   18
"prowess" allowed me to be treated like a "princess." Now whoever was the doorman (last in, first out of the helicopter) offered me a hand. Whoever was the tail and carried the reserve pack always asked if I wanted him to carry anything extra. Whoever saw my skis unloaded before I did would hand them to me. I felt protected. In return I was expected to ski hard. Run after run, as we held up our ends of the unspoken bargain, I began to see heli-skiing as the essence of the whole man/woman thing: Men being their most boyish like to treat women (who can cut it) like girls.

That first night I joined the group I took extra care dressing for   19
dinner. These guys knew I could ski and laugh at their dirty jokes . . . now it was time to identify myself as pure woman. I purposefully picked my pink shirt (prettier) over the blue one with stars (funkier); leggings (sexier) over jeans (jockier). And I chose black flats, no socks over just socks (sloppy) or sneakers (clunky). My hair, which one guy told me he loved because it was so natural (it was a mess! I'll never understand men!), got moussed and sprayed and scrunched until it was unnaturally full and curly; then I tied on a bow and, from my earlobes, hung pink gemstone hearts that matched my shirt. The result: Coco Chanel Goes Skiing.

The group saved me a seat (dinner is family style), and over good   20
food and wine I heard about money-making innovations and miserable marriages, management techniques and dual-career controversies, new restaurants and new reads. By dessert we'd crossed an emotional line equal to the physical one we'd crossed that day—

and created a bond. Little did I know, it would be put to the test the next morning.

The daily rotation had given us the first-group spot. . . . The company photographer, up for the week to shoot pictures for the new brochure, wanted to join our group because 1) we could make perfect turns and 2) we were first out and would take the first untracked lines down the glacier we were headed for. The problem was that our group had no space, so if he were to join, someone would have to drop back to a less skillful group. I realized that I, having no seniority, would be the "guy" to go. 21

Instead a couple of the guys went to the guide room and said, "We've got a great group, no laggers, and we want to keep it intact." No names, nothing. That was that. 22

The sky broke blue that morning, and the first run out we landed in the crease between two peaks on Conrad Glacier. We skied the wide-open glacier most of the morning, then we chopper-hopped over to a run called Scapula for some skiing through trees. "OK, now we'll see if you can ski the tough stuff." With that, Thierry, our guide that day, started down. We followed him around patches of pines until we reached a precariously steep mountainside hugged by trees so huge they left little ski space between them. "Get partners and stick together," he said. "I'll go down and make the left border; over there several hundred meters is a drop—that's your right border. I'll wait at the bottom." And he was off, yodeling so we could hear the right direction. 23

Just before I felt like the uncoordinated, unpopular third-grade kid who's always last picked for the team, Reb, the best of the bunch, picked me. (Skier's etiquette precluded me from choosing him, because he's better than I and I would slow his run.) "I'll follow you," he said. Okay. Go for it. 24

I took a breath and shoved off. Fast. Hard. Straight down, no traverses. Feel it. Don't think it. Tight. One turn after another, and another. Breathe. Ducking, dodging branches. In the air. Turn again, again, again. Breathe. Faster. He's on my tail. Go, give it all you've got. Now. More. Keep it up. Another turn and another. And then I fell, skis skewed to avoid tumbling into a tree well. He fell too but only to avoid crashing into me. Practically gasping for air, I looked over, a "sorry" on my face. Smiling, he said, "Thanks, that was the best of the week." 25

Though I knew he'd have made the whole run (and knew he   26
knew it too) if he'd gone with someone else, he meant what he said.
It was a great run, maybe not as fast and furious as it might have
been, but it was great in another sense: He'd pushed me, I was able
to meet the challenge respectably, and he relished that—and
seemed to take (more than) equal credit for my performance. It was
as though he'd given birth to the skier in me.

The harder I skied the better I got, and I felt the others too took   27
pleasure in my progress. Like when Dave coaxed me over a (huge!)
jump and I made it. Like when Buck, one of the guides, insisted I
carry the reserve pack, knowing I could . . . and I could. Like when
Howard said to follow right behind him, no stopping, top to bottom, and I did. Like when I skied too far below the cutoff to the
helicopter landing and had to climb up a couple hundred feet in a
thigh-deep powder and I did it, and the next runs too, never holding anyone up.

And they took equal pleasure in the idea that I was female, that I   28
would wear a pink bow in my hair and hearts in my ears. What had
first rendered me a pariah, the notion that I was a city woman
whose idea of enjoying the outdoors was to open my window, finally tipped the scale to achieve in the most perfect wilderness a
perfect balance between the sexes.

A Second Look

1 Ettlinger begins with a description of a particular skiing experience.
   When do you begin to see what her true subject will be? Should she
   have indicated it earlier? Why or why not?

2 One way in which Ettlinger shows, rather than tells, her readers what
   happens is by using lively verbs and accurate, interesting adjectives.
   Pick out several examples.

3 The writer uses at least two levels of language in this essay: fairly formal
   and very informal. Pick out examples of both. Why do you think she
   mixes these levels? Do you feel that this technique is effective? Why or
   why not?

4 How does Ettlinger attack the locker-room prejudice of the other skiers?

5 Ettlinger says she became "one of the guys" while keeping her identity
   "as pure woman." Do you agree, or do you think she went against her
   own standards of feminine behavior? Explain.

Ideas for Writing

1 Reread paragraphs 3 and 25. Notice how Ettlinger describes action. Try writing a paragraph or two of your own describing a short period of rapid, intense action such as that of skiing, skating, running, or gymnastics.

2 Tell of an experience in which you were accepted by a group that formerly had excluded you. Tell your readers exactly what the group was, why it excluded you, and what you did to gain acceptance into it.

3 Marjorie Franco and Catherine Ettlinger both write about platonic friendships, but they differ in their description of how these friendships are formed. In a paragraph or two, summarize the differences in their points of view.

Significant Other

Rick Weiss

Looking Forward

Rick Weiss, a writer living in New York City, is married to Natalie Angier, science reporter for *The New York Times*. In this essay, Weiss describes how he and his wife-to-be began competing even before they met, how they made accommodations for their two careers, and how he came to accept a role that at first seemed very strange to him.

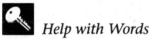 *Help with Words*

harried *(paragraph 3):* disturbed, under stress

cachet *(paragraph 4):* distinction, mark of quality

prestigious *(paragraph 5):* distinguished, impressive

relinquishment *(paragraph 6):* yielding, giving up something

precluded *(paragraph 6):* prevented

anarchist *(paragraph 8):* radical, revolutionary

indoctrinated *(paragraph 8):* taught, trained

accolades *(paragraph 10):* honors, tributes

mantles *(paragraph 10):* cloaks or coverings; here, used as a figure of speech

accouterment *(paragraph 11):* pieces of equipment, accessory

penumbral *(paragraph 11):* shadowy

placid *(paragraph 12):* calm

vapid *(paragraph 12):* dull, without imagination

unabridged *(paragraph 16):* complete

aspiration *(paragraph 16):* ambition, desire

M y wife and I will probably never agree on the way I intro- 1
duced myself on that spring day, during a coffee break at
National Institutes of Health conference.

In my memory it was friendly, something like, "Hey, congratula- 2
tions on getting the job at The Times." But she remembers the greeting as less than cordial: "Hi, I'm Rick Weiss. You got my job."

Moreover, she claims (and she may be right about this) that I 3
added, "And from the look of how harried you are, I'm not really
jealous."

The fact is, she was a bit of a wreck. It was her first month on the 4
job—a much sought after science-writing position for which I and
others had competed. That day the story was big, her deadline was
approaching, and she couldn't find a phone jack for her laptop's
modem. In contrast, I was working for a weekly magazine and
wasn't under pressure; my deadline was four days away. But my
relaxed pace came with a price. No matter how well written, my
article would never carry the cachet of hers. And her paycheck, I
supposed, would make mine look like a drugstore coupon.

Whether or not I let slip a touch of envy, our introduction marked 5
the start of some serious soul-searching on my part. The bottom line
is, I'm one of those guys whose wife has the more prestigious job.
She's a big-time journalist, writing stories I wanted to write myself.

What's more, my falling in love with this hotshot competitor was 6
only the beginning of a slippery slope of professional and personal
relinquishment. Because she lived in New York and I in Washington, we became weekend regulars on the Metroliner. But an allergy
to the mildew in my swampy basement quickly precluded her from
visiting, and it was I who had to elbow my way through Friday
evening crowds at Union Station and, worse, stumble through Penn
Station every Monday morning at 6 for the train back to Washington.

When it became clear we'd have to rearrange our lives to accom- 7
modate our love, it was I who gave up my job and relocated to
Manhattan, where a depressed publishing market forced me to take
a corporate job that left me in journalistic obscurity.

So what's the big deal? After all, I grew up in the 60s and spent 8
my formative years in California in a 25-member anarchist com-
mune that left me well indoctrinated in feminist principles. In those

days, even armed revolution seemed an appropriate means of securing for working women their proper place in the power structure.

Besides, I'm basically a self-assured person with a good sense of humor. So I've been able to shrug a lot of this off with what's become a standard joke: "She's got the job, but I've got her."

But it's not that simple. As the only boy in a Jewish family, I grew up believing I'd inherited a virtual guarantee of special standing. And as an adult things have pretty much gone my way, never forcing me to put my politically correct training to the test. So sure, I got the girl, but it seemed unfair that she got me and everything else—prestige, money and public accolades. It's as though her snagging that job was the first of several lessons the universe figured I was owed—lessons about letting go of traditional mantles of power and discovering new and subtle sources of security as a man.

Now, when attending dinners related to my wife's work, I find myself more quiet than before, wondering whether I'm seen by others as a mere accouterment to my better-known partner. I find myself sympathizing with women at our table who I might previously have written off as "wives." I see that they, like me, have talents and accomplishments of their own—a truth I was not totally blind to before, but one that I couldn't fully appreciate until I entered the penumbral world of "the spouse."

Sometimes, out of defensiveness, I make the problem worse. Rather than offer clues about my skills and interests, I perform a silent experiment in sexual role reversal, in which I patiently wait to see whether anyone will bother asking me what I do or what I think. And again I discover new sympathy for my placid female counterparts, whose quiet smiles, I realize, may be more righteous than vapid.

But my newfound empathy for the mates of public figures is only part of the lesson of my current station in life. The bigger challenge has been to see through society's tradition emblems of power—fame and fortune—and abandon them for a more profound sense of self-confidence and self-worth.

At first I found solace in predictable harbors. At home I took heart in my ability to repair light switches, install shelves and fix the shower faucet, while maintaining firm control over anything having to do with lawyers or accountants. And to retain the respect of fellow writers, I made a point of writing freelance articles for respected publications.

But over time it has become clear that power substitutes are only   15
substitutes. With an appliance repaired here, an article published
there, the contest would have been endless and I'd have found
no peace.

So lately I've been experimenting with a new approach, embrac-   16
ing the unabridged, wretched and remarkable truth of who I am,
and also who I am not—what Zorba called "the whole catastrophe." That angle isn't new, of course. But it's difficult to really let go
of power until you feel the deep fatigue that comes with trying to
hold onto it—and until you accept the notion that an aspiration to
excellence need not be a contest with winners and losers.

Recently I had the opportunity to test whether I had made any   17
progress along these lines, when my wife was awarded a Pulitzer
Prize for her writing at The Times. My heart flip-flopped when she
called with the news; yes, there was a pang of jealousy, but most
of all I was overjoyed about the recognition that she so clearly
had earned.

Hailing a cab to go crosstown for a glass of champagne, I took   18
pleasure in my heart's ratio of pride and envy. And recognizing,
too, that I had not transcended competitiveness altogether, I braced
myself for the speeches I knew her editors would give, congratulat-
ing themselves for the good judgment they showed in choosing to
hire her.

 A Second Look

1 What changes did Weiss make "to accommodate our love"?

2 Weiss states that he was "well indoctrinated in feminist principles."
   Why, then, did he find it hard to accept that his wife had a more prestigious job and a larger salary than he did? How does he finally come to
   terms with this problem?

3 At the time he is writing, is his adjustment to this situation complete?
   How do we know?

4 Where would you place Weiss's essay on a scale running from very
   informal to very formal. Explain your answer.

5 What kind of reading audiences do you think Weiss is writing for? Why
   do you think so?

Ideas for Writing

1 In one paragraph, summarize Weiss's attitude toward traditional gender roles at the time he met his wife-to-be.

2 Describe an experience in which you felt that you did not truly belong with a group but were there as just a wife, husband, brother, sister, or friend. Explain to your readers what the situation was, how you felt, and how you tried to cope or make yourself more comfortable.

3 Weiss writes that he is modern in his thinking, "indoctrinated in feminist principles," and self-assured. Yet for a time he finds it difficult to accept his own and his wife's personal and professional positions. Describe a situation in your own life when a firmly held belief has been challenged by a personal situation.

Women Wasted

Jennifer Bitner

Looking Forward

In this student essay, Jennifer Bitner considers the differences among three generations of women. As she looks at her grandmother, her mother, and herself, she wonders whether the two older women ever felt as she does now.

 Help with Words

aspirations *(paragraph 4):* wishes, ambitions
immersed *(paragraph 5):* totally involved

She sits in the living room of my aunt's house surrounded by blurry colors and shapeless movements. Noises come to her through layers of cotton. Ninety-five years have made her crumple and sag. She is a dying old creature.

She seems so happy; she smiles and hugs me to her softly. Her glassy eyes search out the blur that is my face and kiss it, missing my mouth, but giving me a wonderful nose kiss. In a way, her warm presence is comforting to me, but it also frightens me.

What is there to connect me to this strange old woman who lives strongly in the past, while I am searching for a future? What could I possibly share with someone so old, so near death? Was there any fun, any joy, in her life spent serving husband and children? When I look at an old picture of my grandmother, strange feelings come over me. I have a beautiful picture showing her at about my age.

191

Her hair is pulled back in a soft bun, and her eyes are warm and proud. Her mouth is curved in my smile. I look like the woman in the picture, yet she is so far from the dying woman in the E-Z Boy rocker, and both are far from me.

If I could talk to the girl in the picture, would she be like me? Did 4 she have many dreams? I am sure she dreamed of more than this. She must have had aspirations beyond motherhood, though she probably was not nearly as ambitious as I am. She was a woman at a time when woman meant wife and mother.

Fear hits me, the same fear I feel when I watch my mother clean 5 the house or make my father's dinner. She is so immersed in these simple tasks, as if in a trance. I love these women, but my body and mind cry out that I will not be like them. I cannot confine myself to mindless tasks and unending service.

These women missed so much playing the role of wife and 6 mother. Neither went to college; both stayed home and cared for children and house. They do not know what they missed out on— do they?

Does my mother ever get a vague feeling of distress? At night 7 does she think, "Who am I and what have I done for myself? Where was *my* life in this tangle of years?"

Grandmother is too old to cry for. She smiles and in her semi- 8 senility is content, but I cry for my mother. The only job she ever held was as a secretary. Her life was spent in marriage and raising children. I know she gets depressed sometimes. Does she realize she has a mind she is wasting?

I cry for my mother, and her mother, and for all of the women 9 who have been wasted. Minds, wonderful minds, wasted on dishes and hours of boredom. All of these things I think as I hug this old woman and hear the chatter of my mother in the next room gossiping.

A Second Look

1 One of the writer's strengths is her ability to give us clear pictures of people in just a few sentences. What details help us see what kind of women her grandmother and her mother are?

2 In paragraphs 2 and 5, Bitner says she feels fear. What is she afraid of? Why doesn't she express her fear more directly?

3 What is the writer's attitude toward the traditional role of women? What details indicate this attitude? Do you agree or disagree with her? Why?

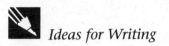

Ideas for Writing

1 Perhaps you disagree with Jennifer Bitner's view of the role of wife and mother. (Review your answer to "A Second Look," question 3.) If so, write a paper in which you give the advantages of a woman's remaining in the home to care for her family. You may wish to list both negative and positive aspects, but your main idea will be that there are still good reasons for a woman to choose the traditional role of wife and mother. If your instructor wishes, you could first discuss the topic in small groups in class.

2 If you are a woman reading this essay, you may feel as Bitner does when you compare yourself to your mother, aunts, grandmothers, or other older women in your family. If so, write a paper in which you describe their attitudes and yours, explaining the differences between them. You might consider Bitner's question: "They do not know what they missed out on—do they?"

3 If you are a man reading this essay, you may be able to look at your father and grandfather and view the situation from their side. Do men of earlier generations have regrets—too much time spent at work and not enough at home, too many years when their children grew up almost without their noticing, too little time spent with their wives? If you think your life will be different, describe what those differences will be. In other words, write about Jennifer Bitner's topic from a male point of view.

Making Connections

Marjorie Franco writes that one difficulty in forming relationships is pressure from outside. This is true whether the relationships are personal or professional: in forming affiliations, we are often influenced by what others think. As Franco puts it: "It's easier to be what others expect us to be."

In the selections in this unit, some of the women conform to what others expect of them, and some do not. Which women belong in which category? Considering what happens to these women, do you agree that "it's easier to be what others expect us to be?" Is the situation different for men?

The Environment

Making Peace with the Planet

Barry Commoner

Looking Forward

Making Peace with the Planet is a book written to help readers understand the problems our human activities are creating in the natural environment. Throughout the book, Commoner explains scientific concepts using language the general reader can understand. This chapter focuses especially on defining the term *global warming*. Notice the ways Commoner tries to alert the reader to the seriousness of the problem.

 Help with Words

exempt *(paragraph 1):* free from, not subject to

breached *(paragraph 2):* broken, penetrated

unwitting *(paragraph 2):* unintended

portending *(paragraph 3):* foretelling, indicating in advance

fluctuating *(paragraph 3):* changing constantly

Sorcerer's Apprentice *(paragraph 3):* a magician's assistant who accidentally released uncontrollable destructive forces while trying to perform the magic feats of his master (a character from an old folk tale)

potentially *(paragraph 3):* capable of being or becoming

mundane *(paragraph 4):* ordinary

overt *(paragraph 4):* open to view

esoteric *(paragraph 4):* understood by only a few

noxious *(paragraph 4):* poisonous

carcinogenic *(paragraph 4):* cancer causing

niches *(paragraph 4):* places, positions

constituents *(paragraph 5):* elements

induce *(paragraph 6):* bring about

geological transformation *(paragraph 7):* physical change

photosynthesis *(paragraph 7):* the process by which plants manufacture food from organic materials, using the sun as the source of energy

global habitat *(paragraph 7):* the earth as a place to live

cataclysmic *(paragraph 8):* referring to a sudden and violent action that produces change in the earth's surface

P eople live in two worlds. Like all living things, we inhabit the natural world, created over the Earth's 5-billion-year history by physical, chemical and biological processes. The other world is our own creation: homes, cars, farms, factories, laboratories, food, clothing, books, paintings, music, poetry. We accept responsibility for events in our own world, but not for what occurs in the natural one. Its storms, droughts, and floods are "acts of God," free of human control and exempt from our responsibility.   1

Now, on a planetary scale, this division has been breached. With the appearance of a continent-sized hole in the Earth's protective ozone layer and the threat of global warming, even droughts, floods, and heat waves may become unwitting acts of man.   2

Like the Creation, the portending global events are cosmic: they change the relationship between the planet Earth and its star, the sun. The sun's powerful influence on the Earth is exerted by two forces: gravity and solar radiation. Gravity is a nearly steady force that fixes the planet's path around the sun. Solar radiation—largely visible and ultraviolet light—is a vast stream of energy that bathes the Earth's surface, fluctuating from day to night and season to season. Solar energy fuels the energy-requiring processes of life; it creates the planet's climate and governs the gradual evolution and the current behavior of its huge and varied population of living things. We have been tampering with this powerful force, unaware, like the Sorcerer's Apprentice, of the potentially disastrous consequences of our actions.   3

We have become accustomed to the now mundane image of the Earth as seen from the first expedition to the moon—a beautiful   4 blue sphere decorated by swirls of fleecy clouds. It is a spectacularly natural object; at that distance, no overt signs of human activity are visible. But this image, now repeatedly thrust before us in photographs, posters, and advertisements, is misleading. Even if the global warming catastrophe never materializes, and the ozone hole remains an esoteric, polar phenomenon, already human activity has profoundly altered global conditions in ways that may not register on the camera. Everywhere in the world, there is now radioactivity that was not there before, the dangerous residue of nuclear explosions and the nuclear power industry; noxious fumes of smog blanket every major city; carcinogenic synthetic pesticides have been detected in mother's milk all over the world; great forests have been cut down, destroying ecological niches and their resident species.

As it reaches the Earth's surface, solar radiation is absorbed and sooner or later converted to heat. The amount of solar radiation that falls on the Earth and of the heat that escapes it depends not only on the daily turning of the Earth and the yearly change of the seasons, but also on the status of the thin gaseous envelope that surrounds the planet. One of the natural constituents of the outer layer of Earth's gaseous skin—the stratosphere—is ozone, a gas made of three oxygen atoms (ordinary oxygen is made of two atoms). Ozone absorbs much of the ultraviolet light radiated from the sun and thereby shields the Earth's surface from its destructive effects. Carbon dioxide and several other atmospheric components act like a valve: they are transparent to visible light but hold back invisible infrared radiation. The light that reaches the Earth's surface during the day is converted to heat that radiates outward in the form of infrared energy. Carbon dioxide, along with several other less prominent gases in the air, governs the Earth's temperature by holding back this outward radiation of heat energy. The greater the carbon dioxide content of the atmosphere, the higher the Earth's temperature. Glass has a similar effect, which causes the winter sun to warm a greenhouse; hence, the "greenhouse effect," the term commonly applied to global warming.

These global effects are not new; they have massively altered the condition of the Earth's surface over its long history. For example, because the early Earth lacked oxygen and therefore the ozone shield, it was once so heavily bathed in solar ultraviolet light as to limit living things to dark places; intense ultraviolet radiation can kill living cells and induce cancer. Similarly, analyses of ice (and the entrapped air bubbles) deposited in the Antarctic over the last 150,000 years indicate that the Earth's temperature fluctuated considerably, closely paralleled by changes in the carbon dioxide level.

Changes in the Earth's vegetation can be expected to influence 7 the carbon dioxide content of the atmosphere. Thus, the massive growth of forests some 200 million to 300 million years ago took carbon dioxide out of the air, eventually converting its carbon into the deposits of coal, oil, and natural gas produced by geological transformation of the dying trees and plants. The huge deposits of fossil fuel, the product of millions of years of photosynthesis, remained untouched until coal, and later petroleum and natural gas, were mined and burned, releasing carbon dioxide into the atmosphere. The amounts of these fuels burned to provide human society with energy represent the carbon captured by photosynthesis over millions of years. So, by burning them, in the last 750 years we have returned carbon dioxide to the atmosphere thousands of times faster than the rate at which it was removed by the early tropical forests. The atmosphere's carbon dioxide content has increased by 20 percent since 1850, and there is good evidence that the Earth's average temperature has increased about 1 degree Fahrenheit since then. If nothing is done to change this trend, temperatures may rise by about 2.5 to 10 degrees more in the next fifty years. This is about the same change in temperature that marked the end of the last ice age about 15,000 years ago—an event that drastically altered the global habitat. If the new, man-made warming occurs, there will be equally drastic changes, this time endangering a good deal of the world that people have fashioned for themselves. Polar ice will melt and the warmer oceans will expand, raising the sea level and flooding many cities; productive agricultural areas, such as the U.S. Midwest, may become deserts; the weather is likely to become more violent.

Regardless of how serious the resultant warming of the Earth 8 turns out to be, and what, if anything, can be done to avoid its cataclysmic effects, it demonstrates a basic fact: that in the short span of its history, human society has exerted an effect on its planetary habitat that matches the size and impact of the natural processes that until now solely governed the global condition.

A Second Look

1 According to Commoner, what accounts for peoples' unwillingness to take responsibility for environmental problems such as global warming?

2 To help the reader understand the dangerous changes that are taking place in the natural environment, Commoner defines many scientific terms as he writes. For example, in paragraph 3 he explains what he means by cosmic global events by saying: "they change the relationship between the planet Earth and its star, the sun." Point out other examples of definitions that clarify.

3 Read paragraph 5 carefully, and then restate what causes the "greenhouse effect" in your own words.

4 What evidence does Commoner give that global warming is a real possibility?

5 If you were to answer the question totally honestly, would you say that you are or are not concerned about the ozone layer and global warming? Do you feel responsible for making changes to control the problem? How do you explain these attitudes?

 *Ideas for Writing*

Write an essay in which you urge the people who live in your town or your neighborhood to take action on some environmental problem. Start by describing what the problem is and what negative consequences it will produce. For example, you might write about an oil company that is polluting a nearby stream, a lumber company that is cutting timber from surrounding hillsides, or a problem that people in the neighborhood contribute directly to, such as littering in a certain location.

As you write, try to help your readers understand exactly what causes the problem and how they can help solve it. Remember that you need to convince the readers that they are responsible for the natural environment.

A Fable for Tomorrow

Rachel Carson

Looking Forward

"A Fable for Tomorrow" was published in the 1960s as the first chapter of Carson's book, *Silent Spring*, which warns of the consequences of the uncontrolled use of pesticides. During the past thirty years, the book has become a classic that has greatly influenced the environmental movement in the United States.

 ### *Help with Words*

viburnum *(paragraph 2):* a flowering shrub
maladies *(paragraph 3):* illnesses
stricken *(paragraph 3):* made seriously ill
moribund *(paragraph 4):* dying
specter *(paragraph 9):* ghost

here was once a town in the heart of America where all life 1
seemed to live in harmony with its surroundings. The town lay in the midst of a checkerboard of prosperous farms, with fields of grain and hillsides of orchards where, in spring, white clouds of bloom drifted above the green fields. In autumn, oak and maple and birch set up a blaze of color that flamed and flickered across a back-

drop of pines. The foxes barked in the hills and deer silently crossed the fields, half hidden in the mists of the fall mornings.

Along the roads, laurel, viburnum and alder, great ferns and 2 wildflowers delighted the traveler's eye through much of the year. Even in winter the roadsides were places of beauty, where countless birds came to feed on the berries and on the seed heads of the dried weeds rising above the snow. The countryside was, in fact, famous for the abundance and variety of its bird life, and when the flood of migrants was pouring through in spring and fall people traveled from great distances to observe them. Others came to fish the streams, which flowed clear and cold out of the hills and contained shady pools where trout lay. So it had been from the days many years ago when the first settlers raised their houses, sank their wells, and built their barns.

Then a strange blight crept over the area and everything began to 3 change. Some evil spell had settled on the community: mysterious maladies swept the flocks of chickens; the cattle and sheep sickened and died. Everywhere was a shadow of death. The farmers spoke of much illness among their families. In the town the doctors had become more and more puzzled by new kinds of sickness appearing among their patients. There had been several sudden and unexplained deaths, not only among adults but even among children, who would be stricken suddenly while at play and die within a few hours.

There was a strange stillness. The birds, for example—where had 4 they gone? Many people spoke of them, puzzled and disturbed. The feeding stations in the backyards were deserted. The few birds seen anywhere were moribund; they trembled violently and could not fly. It was a spring without voices. On the mornings that had once throbbed with the dawn chorus of robins, catbirds, doves, jays, wrens, and scores of other bird voices there was now no sound; only silence lay over the fields and woods and marsh.

On the farms the hens brooded, but no chicks hatched. The farm- 5 ers complained that they were unable to raise any pigs—the litters were small and the young survived only a few days. The apple trees were coming into bloom but no bees droned among the blossoms, so there was no pollination and there would be no fruit.

The roadsides, once so attractive, were now lined with browned 6 and withered vegetation as though swept by fire. These, too, were silent, deserted by all living things. Even the streams were now life-less. Anglers no longer visited them, for all the fish had died.

In the gutters under the eaves and between the shingles of the roofs, a white granular powder still showed a few patches; some weeks before it had fallen like snow upon the roofs and the lawns, the fields and streams. 7

No witchcraft, no enemy action had silenced the rebirth of new life in this stricken world. The people had done it themselves. 8

This town does not actually exist, but it might easily have a thousand counterparts in America or elsewhere in the world. I know of no community that has experienced all the misfortunes I describe. Yet every one of these disasters has actually happened somewhere, and many real communities have already suffered a substantial number of them. A grim specter has crept upon us almost unnoticed, and this imagined tragedy may easily become a stark reality we all shall know. 9

What has already silenced the voices of spring in countless towns in America? 10

A Second Look

1 One reason Carson's fable is effective is her use of vivid, specific words. To illustrate the importance of the word choice, try rereading paragraph 1 omitting all the specific words or substituting general words for the specific ones. How much information is left?

2 The mood and tone of the fable change suddenly in paragraph 3. Pick out three examples of word choice that help Carson shift to a fearful or frightening tone.

3 Mention several examples of the changes that have made this a *silent* spring.

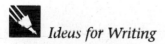 *Ideas for Writing*

In a short descriptive essay, describe the effects of pollution that you have seen. If possible, visit the scene again, and list specific details that will help make the scene vivid and real to the reader. As you view the scene, try to imagine how the situation will be in twenty years if nothing is done to stop the pollution.

The Balance of Nature

Edward Goldsmith and Others

Looking Forward

The authors of this essay provide several examples of the harm that results from any disturbance to the balance of nature. All creatures, even those that are deadly pests to man, have a role in natural processes. The authors warn about the possibility of disaster as a result of man's continued tampering with and destruction of the world's ecosystems.

 Help with Words

eradicate *(paragraph 1):* eliminate
ombarked *(paragraph 1):* started
rife *(paragraph 3):* widespread
unabated *(paragraph 3):* without stopping
extract *(paragraph 4):* obtain
haphazard *(paragraph 5):* random
zooplankton *(paragraph 6):* small animal organisms that float in water
decomposers *(paragraph 6):* organisms that cause decay
photosynthesizing *(paragraph 7):* making food from organic materials
proliferate *(paragraph 8):* reproduce
gossamer *(paragraph 9):* silky, sheer
disarray *(paragraph 9):* confusion
inevitably *(paragraph 10):* certainly, unavoidably
resilience *(paragraph 12):* adaptability

I n the 1960s, in an attempt to eradicate malaria, the World   1
Health Organization embarked on a major campaign to rid the
tropics of the mosquitoes that carry the disease. Borneo was to be
one of the regions cleared, and a massive spraying campaign was
initiated throughout the worst affected areas. The chosen pesticide
was DDT, a highly toxic and cancer-causing chemical since banned
in most western countries but still widely used in the Third World.

Initially the programme was successful and the mosquito popu-   2
lation fell dramatically. But it was not only mosquitoes that died.
Numerous other species were poisoned by the DDT, among them a
minute wasp that preyed upon caterpillars living in the thatch of
local houses. With the wasp gone, the caterpillar numbers increased
to plague proportions, devouring the roofs of houses and causing
them to collapse. Nonetheless, the spraying programme continued.
The dead mosquitoes were eaten by gecko lizards which, as they
became sick, proved easy prey for the local cats. As a result the cats
accumulated large quantities of DDT, passed on from insect to liz-
ard to cat. The cats began to die in their thousands—and the local
population of rats exploded. The rats not only ate local crops but
brought an even greater menace—bubonic plague. In desperation
the Borneo government called for cats to be parachuted into the
worst affected regions.

Today, the mosquitoes have returned to the sprayed areas and   3
malaria is still rife. Many pesticides are now ineffective, the mosquitoes having developed resistance to them. But, as in other parts of
the world, the spraying goes on unabated. And the subtle balance of
nature continues to be disrupted.

All Things Connect

"No man is an island, entire of it self," wrote the Elizabethan poet   4
John Donne. And so it is with the species of plants and animals that
make up the natural world. None can survive in isolation. To eat,
the lion must prey on the gazelle, the gazelle must graze on grass,
and the grass must extract nutrients from the soil. And all are de-
pendent on the Sun, without whose energy there would be little life
on Earth.

The natural world is thus much more than a haphazard collection ₅
of plants and animals. The food chain that links one organism to
another binds each into an interdependent community—or ecosystem—in which all living creatures, however small, have their place
and function. At the bottom of the food chain are the green plants—
flowering plants, ferns, mosses, seaweed and microscopic algae.
These primary producers take carbon dioxide from the atmosphere
and water from the soil and use the radiant energy from the Sun to
produce energy-rich glucose, a type of sugar. In the process, they
release oxygen into the atmosphere, without which plants and animals would be unable to survive.

Feeding on the primary producers are plant-eaters or her- ₆
bivores—on land, deer, kangaroos, rabbits, caterpillars and the like,
in the oceans, microscopic animals of the zooplankton, which graze
on the tiny algae. These plant-eating primary consumers are preyed
upon by meat-eating secondary consumers, who themselves are
preyed upon by the larger meat-eaters such as the big cats, birds of
prey and sharks at the top of the food chain. Meanwhile, decomposers, such as bacteria and fungi, break down dead matter, recycling its nutrients through the ecosystem. Bacteria and fungi also
play a crucial role in dissolving minerals out of rocks, making the
minerals available to plants and animals.

While green plants "breathe in" carbon dioxide and release oxy- ₇
gen when they are photosynthesizing, primary and secondary consumers inhale oxygen and release carbon dioxide. This kind of give-
and-take exchange between one living organism and another is a
fundamental feature of the natural world. . . .

The Web of Life

The complex interrelationships between plants and animals in the ₈
ecosystem are critical to its stability. They ensure that the flow of
energy through the system is kept constant, that nutrients are available, and that waste products are recycled. Although over time, individual species may change through evolution, with some disap-
pearing altogether, while new species appear and proliferate, the
overall system is kept in balance. . . .

Yet, the more we learn of the workings of the natural world, the ₉
clearer it becomes that there is a limit to the disruption that the
environment can endure. Like the gossamer threads of a spider's

web, an ecosystem can only take so much stress and only repair so much damage. Sever a vital link in the food chain and the ecosystem is thrown into disarray. Destroy an insect's natural predators and the insect's numbers will explode—often to pest proportions—before a balance is restored. Disrupt the recycling of nutrients and the whole ecosystem will begin to decay. . . .

Unseen Extinctions

Although most attention has focused on the 'cuddlier' animals un- 10
der threat—cuddly if only because they make good children's toys and excellent photographs—our fate, and that of millions of other species, is likely to depend more on the survival of insects and plants than pandas or leopards. For, important as pandas and leopards are, their loss would not have the same impact as the insect pollinators or decomposers. Without decomposers, for example, the nutrient cycles within ecosystems would be fatally disrupted, depriving the soil of its fertility. Inevitably, given the role that biological organisms play in regulating the chemical composition of the atmosphere, climatic patterns would also be affected.

As one species follows another into extinction, so a chain reaction 11
is triggered. With 50 species currently being lost every day, some warn that we are on the brink of mass extinction. . . .

The resilience of nature is being stretched to the limit. Wherever 12
we care to look we can see the devastation caused by our activities and the disruption of one ecosystem after another. The greenhouse effect, the death of marine mammals, the die-back of trees throughout Europe and North America, the disruption of global climate all provide clear warnings that the natural world is sick. It may take very little more before the life-support systems on which we humans depend are finally overwhelmed.

 A Second Look

1 The authors of this essay want to emphasize the changes in nature that are brought about by man. Therefore, much of the essay is organized from cause to effect. Examine paragraphs 1, 2, and 3 carefully, and name each cause and the effect that resulted from it.

2 In order to make scientific concepts clear to the general reader, the authors often define terms as they introduce them. Locate the definition of "ecosystem," and then give an example of an ecosystem.

3 The first subheading of the essay is entitled "All Things Connect." What examples do the authors use to show how things in nature connect?

4 Why is the extinction of species of insects and plants even more important than that of larger animals?

Ideas for Writing

1 An important tool for writing (and learning) is the summary. When you are writing a summary of someone else's work, you leave out most details and include only those that seem absolutely necessary to explain the main points. Moreover, you should do this using primarily your words, not quoting directly from the original writer. With these guidelines in mind, write a one-paragraph summary of the first three paragraphs of this essay. When you have finished, change papers with a classmate. Read his or her summary, and decide whether it is accurate and clear. If not, how might it be improved? Your classmate will do the same with your summary.

2 Some environmental problems can be solved only by scientists or governments. Others, however, can be solved or at least improved by ordinary citizens. Write an essay suggesting ways that everyone in your neighborhood or town can work to improve the environment. Brainstorm, either by yourself or with classmates, to think of problems and solutions in your area. Then choose one or two for your essay. Be as specific as possible.

Generalizations like "We should work in every way we can to improve the environment" will not do. Most people agree with that already.

Final Warning

Robert Peter Gale and Thomas Hauser

Looking Forward

The city of Chernobyl lies in Ukraine, formerly part of the Soviet Union. Early in the morning of April 26, 1986, Chernobyl gained sudden and awful fame as the site of the worst nuclear accident in history. Dr. Robert Peter Gale was later invited to visit the city to help those that survived this disaster. Afterward, he recorded his experiences and shared his reflections on nuclear danger in a book written with Thomas Hauser, *Final Warning: The Legacy of Chernobyl*. In this excerpt, Gale and Hauser give some background and describe what happened on that April morning.

Help with Words

virtually *(paragraph 2):* almost totally

devoid *(paragraph 2):* empty, barren

endeavors *(paragraph 3):* attempts, enterprises

painstakingly *(paragraph 3):* carefully, precisely

malfunctions *(paragraph 3):* breakdowns, problems

moderator *(paragraph 5):* substance used in a nuclear reactor to slow down neutrons

diminishing *(paragraph 7):* reducing, making smaller

cladding *(paragraph 8):* covering

plume *(paragraph 8):* a featherlike shape, as of smoke or gas

dispersing *(paragraph 8):* scattering

adjacent *(paragraph 8):* adjoining, nearby

bitumen *(paragraph 11):* substance used to waterproof roofs; often used as a synonym for *asphalt* or *pitch*

213

T hree centuries before Christopher Columbus sighted land 1
in the Americas, long before the Renaissance and Reforma-
tion changed Europe, five hundred years before Peter the Great extended the Russian Empire, the town of Chernobyl was founded.
For eight hundred years, its people lived off the land, harvesting rye
and potatoes, breeding cattle and hogs. The soil was sandy, and
much of the surrounding area was marshland unsuited for farming.
Still, the village lived on. Napoleon and Hitler invaded Russia and
failed. Through famine, plague, and bitter-cold winters, the people
of Chernobyl held their ground.

Now Chernobyl is virtually deserted, devoid of human life, sur- 2
rounded by a silent brown forest. It is one of 179 towns and settle-
ments evacuated in the wake of the worst nuclear accident in history. The men, women, and children who lived there have been told
that their homes will be uninhabitable for years to come.

Nuclear power is an unforgiving technology; it allows little room 3
for error. Proponents and opponents alike agree that the nuclear
industry cannot tolerate the same risks as other industrial endeavors. A single accident can change the world. Thus, nuclear
power plants are painstakingly designed, regularly tested, and
equipped with numerous back-up safety devices. The men and
women responsible for their existence are, for the most part, sincere,
dedicated, intelligent individuals, and the safety of the reactor
is their primary concern. However, even at the highest levels of
technological expertise, failures occur. People make mistakes.
Machines break. And over the years, nuclear power plants have
endured thousands of malfunctions—some minor, others not so
small. . . .

Every nuclear power plant system carries the potential for fail- 4
ure. Malfunctions can result from errors in design, manufacture,
installation, maintenance, or day-to-day operation. Sabotage, earth-
quakes, tornados, and other natural phenomena carry equal potential for disaster. Brown's Ferry and Three Mile Island were two re-
minders. Comparable incidents at Detroit Edison's Fermi Unit
Number 1 and various nuclear power plants around the world un-
derscore safety concerns. Still, no one died at Three Mile Island. No

radiation was released into the atmosphere at Brown's Ferry. And as the years passed, many observers began to question whether the "dangers" of nuclear power were real or imagined. Then came Chernobyl. . . .

The pride of the Soviet nuclear program was a planned six-unit 5 complex at Chernobyl. Chernobyl Unit Number 1 went into service in 1977, and was followed by Units 2, 3, and 4 in 1978, 1981, and 1983 respectively. Units 5 and 6 were scheduled to come on line in 1988. The Chernobyl reactors were similar to one another in design, but differed from units in the United States in two significant respects. First, rather than using water as a moderator, the Chernobyl units employed graphite. And as a consequence of this and several other design features, chain reactions within the reactor were more likely to run out of control in the event of a loss-of-coolant accident. And second, while the Chernobyl units were protected by strong walls, they were housed in buildings which lacked reinforced concrete domes typical of Western containment structures. Whether either of these factors contributed to the scope of the disaster which ultimately occurred is subject to dispute, given the magnitude of the Chernobyl explosion.

The chain of events leading to disaster began on the morning of 6 April 25, 1986. Unit Number 4 was scheduled to be taken out of service for routine maintenance, and the plant's electrical engineers wanted to conduct a test to determine how long the turbine-generators would continue to produce electricity to run the water pumps necessary to cool the reactor after the normal electrical supply had been interrupted.

At 1:00 A.M., the reactor's power level was lowered to prepare for 7 the test. Then, over the next twenty-four hours, technicians systematically disconnected power regulation and emergency cooling systems which would have automatically shut the reactor down and interfered with the test. Finally, at 1:23 on the morning of April 26, 1986—twenty-four hours after preparation for the test had begun— the flow of steam to the turbine was halted. Almost immediately, the cooling pumps slowed, diminishing the flow of cooling water to the reactor core. Normally, at this point, the reactor would have shut down, but the automatic shutdown system was one of six safety mechanisms that had been deliberately disconnected. Within seconds, there was a massive heat buildup in the reactor core, triggering an uncontrollable chain reaction. Power surged. At 1:23 A.M., the Unit Number 4 reactor exploded.

There were two blasts, three seconds apart. The first was caused 8 by steam, the second by steam or hydrogen which had formed when the fuel-rod cladding began to melt and interacted with water in the pressure vessel. The reactor core was torn apart. Its thousand-ton cover-plate was propelled upward, causing the building roof above the reactor to collapse. A deadly plume of radioactive material—more than was released at Hiroshima and Nagasaki—shot into the air, forming a fiery image above the roof before dispersing into the atmosphere. Exposed to intense heat and open air, the graphite moderator began to burn. Radioactive water gushed into the reactor hall. Hot chunks of fuel and metal landed on what was left of the building roof and the roofs of adjacent buildings. Thirty fires began to burn.

Within minutes, the nuclear plant's firefighting unit was on the 9 scene—twenty-eight men under the command of Major Leonid Telyatnikov, "You had the impression you could see the radiation," Telyatnikov said later. "There were flashes of light springing from place to place, substances glowing, luminescent, a bit like sparklers."

Telyatnikov ordered a "stage three" alarm, the highest for Soviet 10 firefighters, summoning 250 reserves from as far away as Kiev. Then he and the few men available began working desperately to halt the fires. Their primary concern was that Unit Number 4 shared a ventilation system with, and was housed in the same reactor hall as, Unit Number 3. If the fire spread and Unit 3 went up in flames, the disaster would double in magnitude.

A dozen firemen in the Unit 3 reactor block attacked the blaze 11 with hand-held extinguishers. As that struggle progressed, Telyatnikov led six men up a hundred-foot ladder to the collapsed roof of the reactor hall. Because of the heat, what was left of the asphalt roof had begun to melt. With each step, the firemen's boots sunk into the bitumen, and they had to strain to pull free. Poisonous fumes made breathing difficult; visibility was near zero. Water that was poured on the flames turned instantly to scalding radioactive steam.

Firefighting units from nearby towns began to arrive at three- 12 thirty A.M. Still, the fires raged. "We knew about the radiation," Telyatnikov said later. "We were trying to get the fire before the radiation got us. We are firemen. This is what we were trained for.

We are supposed to fight fires. We knew we must stay to the end. That was our duty."

Shortly before dawn, all fires except one in the Unit 4 reactor core   13 (which would burn for weeks) had been extinguished. The reactor hall was in shambles. Of the seven men who fought the blaze on the building roof, all but Telyatnikov (who was hospitalized for three months) would die as a result of radiation exposure.

AFTERWORD

The nuclear disaster described by Gale and Hauser occurred in 1986. In late 1991, writer Robert Cullen was traveling in Ukraine where he visited the village of Glevakha. An elderly resident, Yevgeny Martynenko, showed him around the village, and they entered the small Orthodox church to observe part of the Sunday service. Cullen writes:

> As we watched, a blond middle-aged woman, weeping quietly, moved among the people, handing out cookies and pieces of candy. She did so, Martynenko said, to mark the first anniversary of the death of her sixteen-year-old son, and to thank the congregation for sharing her grief.
>
> "Why did the boy die so young?" I asked him.
>
> "Brain cancer," Martynenko said. "Chernobyl." It struck me that all across Ukraine, whenever anyone died young, people were explaining the death to themselves with that one word. ("Report from Ukraine," *The New Yorker*, January 27, 1992)

A Second Look

1 Reread paragraph 1. Why do you think the writers begin with this information?

2 Beginning with paragraph 6, Gale and Hauser describe the process by which reactor number 4 overheats and explodes, causing fire and the release of radioactive material. How is this material arranged? Would some other type of organization be more effective?

3 One purpose of this selection is to explain cause and effect. Beginning with the technical information contained in paragraph 5, trace the chain of causes and effects that conclude with the radioactive release (paragraph 8).

4 The final paragraphs focus on Major Telyatnikov and the firefighters. Why do you think the authors concentrate on these men at the conclusion of the selection?

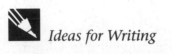 *Ideas for Writing*

1 Using some of your library's reference works (such as *The Reader's Guide*, a newspaper index, or the brief news summaries in *Facts on File*), learn what has happened to the city of Chernobyl and the surrounding towns and villages since the 1986 disaster. Write a summary of the information you find.

2 Using the techniques you have examined in Gale and Hauser's work, write a clear description of the process by which something happens. You may pick what you want to write about. Check to see that all the steps (or causes and effects if that is what you are describing) are in the correct order and that you explain terms or processes your readers might not be familiar with.

Making Connections

1 Barry Commoner's *Making Peace with the Planet*, Rachel Carson's *Silent Spring*, and Edward Goldsmith's "The Balance of Nature" share at least one common purpose: impressing readers with the seriousness of environmental problems. Yet each is quite different from the others in writing style and content. If you were assigned the task of writing an essay to make people feel more responsible for the environment, which of these three selections would you take as a model? What would help you decide?

2 If global warming continues unchecked, there is the possibility that conditions like those at the end of the last ice age could recur. Barry Commoner describes such conditions briefly in paragraph 7 of *Making Peace with the Planet*. Moreover, if nuclear accidents continue, says Robert Peter Gale, large parts of the world could look like the empty and radiation-polluted land around Chernobyl. Write a short fable like Rachel Carson's, and describe what the area where you live would be like if it experienced increased global warming or a large nuclear accident.

Frontiers

Our Brain's Successor

Robert Jastrow

Looking Forward

Robert Jastrow is an astronomer, physicist, author, and university professor. In this look at the future, Dr. Jastrow predicts that a new form of intelligence greater than humanity's will evolve. The human brain may soon become inferior to the artificial intelligence of supercomputers.

 Help with Words

snippet *(paragraph 1):* a small piece
parse *(paragraph 2):* analyze the parts of a sentence, such as subject, verb, direct object, and so forth
competent *(paragraph 2):* adequate
inexhaustible *(paragraph 2):* without limit
prospect *(paragraph 4):* view of something to come
jargon *(paragraph 5):* a specialized or technical language
mammoth *(paragraph 7):* huge
subordinate *(paragraph 7):* inferior to another
enhance *(paragraph 10):* make greater or better
facet *(paragraph 10):* a part

 he following snippet of unrehearsed dialogue took place a   1
few years ago between a computer and a human subject.

Subject: Men are all alike.
Computer: IN WHAT WAY

Subject: They're always bugging me about something or other.
Computer: CAN YOU THINK OF A SPECIFIC EXAMPLE
Subject: Well, my boyfriend made me come here.
Computer: YOUR BOYFRIEND MADE YOU COME HERE
Subject: He says I'm depressed much of the time.
Computer: I AM SORRY TO HEAR YOU ARE DEPRESSED

Computers programmed to parse sentences and carry out natu-   2
ral conversations are little more than parlor games, but they demonstrate an eye-opening level of artificial intelligence to anyone who
thinks these devices are merely fast adding machines. During the
past ten years, machines have taken over a large fraction of clerical
jobs in the United States, such as accounting and inventory control;
computers fill customer orders and manage airline reservations;
and they are beginning to move up into higher levels of management, to make competent decisions on security investments and
marketing strategies. Computers also make excellent teachers. They
can give personal attention to hundreds of students at a time; their
patience is inexhaustible; they are rarely in a hurry to get back to
scholarly research; and they are never sarcastic.

If these trends continue, many jobs in businesses and schools will   3
be filled by computer brains that talk, listen and remember everything. They will be there because they cost less to keep in repair
than human brains, they aren't unionized, and they never get tired.

Most people find this prospect depressing, but even more unset-   4
tling developments are in the works. The latest trends in computer
evolution suggest that the inroads of the intelligent machine will
not stop, even at fairly high-level jobs. For anyone who believes in
the permanent superiority of man over the machine, these trends
are alarming.

Since the birth of the modern computer in the 1950s, computers   5
have increased in power and capability by a factor of ten every
seven years; seven years is a generation in computer evolution, in
the jargon of computer scientists. The first generation of computers
was a billion times clumsier and less efficient than the human brain.
Today, midway between the fourth and fifth generations, electronic
brains are only ten thousand times clumsier than the human brain.
The gap has been narrowed. Around 1995, in the seventh computer
generation, the gap will be closed entirely.

relating or *having a character of theory*

And <u>theoretical</u> physics indicates no early limits to further com- 6
puter growth: Computers, unlike the human brain, do not have to
pass through a birth canal.

As these nonbiological intelligences increase in size and capacity, 7
there will be people around to teach them everything they know.
One sees a vision of mammoth brains in the next century, which
have soaked up the wisdom of the human race and gone on from
there. If this forecast is accurate, man is doomed to a <u>subordinate</u>
status on his own planet.

The story is an old one on the Earth: In the struggle for survival, 8
bigger brains are better. One hundred million years ago, when the
brainy little mammal coexisted with the less intelligent dinosaurs,
the mammal survived and the dinosaur vanished. It appears that in
the next chapter of this unfolding story fate has cast man in the role
of the dinosaur.

What can be done? The answer is obvious: Pull the plug. 9

That may not be so easy. Computers <u>enhance</u> the productivity of 10
human labor; they create wealth and the leisure to enjoy it; they
have <u>ushered</u> in the Golden Age. In fifteen or twenty years, the
brightest and the best of computer brains will be advising top-level
management on every facet of the nation's existence: the economy,
transportation, security, medicine, communications. . . . If someone
pulled the plug, chaos would result. The poor fellow would be
lynched. There is no turning back anymore. . . .

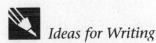

A Second Look

1 What is surprising or unexpected about the dialogue between the human being and the computer in paragraph 1?
2 Why does Jastrow believe that computer intelligence will grow faster
than human intelligence?
3 Since computers are created by people, why can't we control their
development?

Ideas for Writing

1 In paragraph 2, Jastrow states that computers "make excellent
teachers." Have you ever been taught by a computer? If so, compare a

human being and a machine as teachers. First, show how a typical human instructor teaches a lesson and how he or she interacts with students. Then show how a computer does the same job. (Remember to provide a link to help your readers know when you change subjects—from human teacher to computer teacher.) You may assume that many of your readers have not had instruction by computer, so explain clearly what it is like. If you wish to explain which kind of teaching you prefer, you may.

2 Researchers are now experimenting with computers as counselors. You may someday be able to give a computer a description of a personal problem; the computer will then analyze it and print out possible solutions in order of their effectiveness. Would you feel comfortable explaining your problems to a computer and getting advice from it? What would be the advantages and disadvantages? Write a short paper explaining your feelings about going to a computer-counselor.

3 Imagine that you are sitting at the console of the computer-counselor described in the preceding writing topic. You are going to input a personal problem in one or two paragraphs. Remember that the computer cannot help by looking concerned and understanding or by nodding its head and saying, "Yes, I see; well, that's too bad." It is entirely up to you to state your problem briefly, clearly, and completely.

The Answer

Fredric Brown

Looking Forward

In this science fiction story, Fredric Brown creates both suspense and surprise. As you read, notice what details Brown includes so that the reader is
quickly able to imagine the time and setting of the story.

 Help with Words

ceremoniously *(paragraph 1):* formally, very properly
sub-ether *(paragraph 1):* the lower atmosphere
bore *(paragraph 1):* carried
cybernetics machine *(paragraph 2):* an electronic computer

D war Ev ceremoniously soldered the final connection with 1
gold. The eyes of a dozen television cameras watched him
and the sub-ether bore throughout the universe a dozen pictures of
what he was doing.

He straightened and nodded to Dwar Reyn, then moved to a 2
position beside the switch that would complete the contact when he
threw it. The switch that would connect, all at once, all of the mons-
ter computing machines of all the populated planets in the universe—96 billion planets—into the supercircuit that would connect
them all into one super-calculator, one cybernetics machine that
would combine all of the knowledge of the galaxies.

Dwar Reyn spoke briefly to the watching and listening trillions. 3
Then after a moment's silence he said, "Now, Dwar Ev."

Dwar Ev threw the switch. There was a mighty hum, the surge of 4
power from 96 billion planets. Lights flashed and quieted along the
miles-long panel.

Dwar Ev stepped back and drew a deep breath. "The honor of 5
asking the first question is yours, Dwar Reyn."

"Thank you," said Dwar Reyn. "It shall be a question which no 6
single cybernetics machine has been able to answer."

He turned to face the machine. "Is there a God?" 7

The mighty voice answered without hesitation, without the click 8
of a single relay.

"Yes, *now* there is a God." 9

Sudden fear flashed on the face of Dwar Ev. He leaped to grab 10
the switch.

A bolt of lighting from the cloudless sky struck him down and 11
fused the switch shut.

 A Second Look

1 Pick out several details in paragraph 1 that suggest that this event is a
  special occasion.
2 When and where does this event take place? Explain your answer.
3 Why does Dwar Reyn ask the machine if there is a God?
4 What questions does the story raise about man's technological
  ambitions?

Ideas for Writing

Imagine that you are in the television audience watching the ceremony
described in "The Answer." Describe in two or three paragraphs what
happens next. What might the machine-god do or say as it takes over?
Assume that your reader is already familiar with the events that led up to
the bolt of lightning.

A Voyager's Greetings

Linda Salzman Sagan

Looking Forward

In the fall of 1977, the United States launched two unmanned spacecraft, Voyager I and Voyager II, on an exploratory journey to the outer solar system and beyond. On board was information for any intelligent beings who might meet one of the Voyagers beyond our world. There were photographs of Earth and its inhabitants, recorded music (including Bach, Beethoven, and Chuck Berry), and greetings from the Earth spoken in fifty-five languages. Both Voyagers have now passed beyond the boundaries of our solar system. We await an answer to our messages.

Help with Words

gregariousness *(paragraph 1):* friendliness
eloquent *(paragraph 1):* well-spoken
interlocutory *(paragraph 1):* referring to conversation
chasm *(paragraph 3):* canyon, deep gulf
jurisdiction *(paragraph 4):* domain, area of authority
Marco Polo *(paragraph 4):* a famous Italian traveler of the late thirteenth and early fourteenth centuries
emissary *(paragraph 4):* messenger
enticing *(paragraph 5):* tempting
sentient *(paragraph 6):* having senses
effusive *(paragraph 6):* overflowing, unreserved
salutations *(paragraph 7):* greetings
void *(paragraph 9):* empty space
progeny *(paragraph 9):* offspring, descendants

T he Voyager spacecraft hurtling through space as I write   1
these words resembles a glistening cocoon carrying on it a
gold record, a gift to all our intelligent counterparts inhabiting the
universe. The greetings part of the record is a celebration of the human spirit, emphasizing our gregariousness, our joy in being the
social creatures we are, and expressing our desire to be thought of
as eloquent in this, our first speaking engagement to the universe.
We are saying that language is important here, and that we would
welcome—indeed, relish—a dialogue with another interlocutory
civilization elsewhere in the cosmos.

We are Robinson Crusoe on island Earth—inventive, resourceful   2
and creative, but alone. We scan this rim of the horizon for any passing ships that might be sailing the star-encrusted ocean. Hoping to
make contact, we call across the vastness of space; cupping our
hands to our mouth we shout, "Hello out there, is anybody home?"

What if there is no reply? Are we just crying in the wilderness?   3
How sad it would be if our cosmic yoo-hoo echoed through the
canyon of space and reached no one on the other side of the chasm.
All we'd hear would be our own greetings, warm and heartfelt,
sounding as hollow as pennies dropped into a glass jar.

Under a sun-drenched Florida sky, a few hundred people gath-   4
ered, outfitted with special gear for the occasion—sunglasses, bin-
oculars and cameras—to watch Voyager rise from Earth in a blast of
white light, a puff of sunset-colored smoke and a sky-splitting roar.
Watching Voyager flash out of our sight, and eventually out of our
jurisdiction, on its one-way ticket to who-knows-where, one hopes
that, like Marco Polo, it will find itself at the gates of some ancient
and great civilization. As our emissary, it will extend greetings and
present our calling card (or disc, in this case), as any well-mannered
Victorian guest would do when out visiting in the neighborhood.

And what an enticing assortment Voyager is instructed to present   5
to these extraterrestrial hosts, a package of great interest and importance—providing they have ears. Eyes would also be a great help.
But since I'm unable to conceive of an organism that is highly developed intellectually and does not have sense organs, I must adopt
the assumption that such beings will be able to experience Voyager
with both their senses and their intellects.

If you had the opportunity to send a greeting to another sentient   6
being living on another world, what would you convey in the brief
seconds you would be allowed to speak? Would your message be a
general one, expressing good will from everyone here to everyone
there, or would it be a message from you as an individual? Would it
sound like the regards one sends to a distant relation, or would the
tone be warm and effusive? Perhaps you would be most comfortable with a formal greeting, one set in tradition, or would you just
send the basics—"Hi there, we don't bite, what's it like where you
are? Yours truly, Earth."

Essentially, all the elements mentioned are contained in the fifty-   7
five salutations, each one of which is spoken in a different language.
. . . A few of the languages, such as Sumerian, Akkadian and Hittite,
are no longer heard in our modern world, and although Latin is, it is
used primarily for religious or ceremonial occasions; but because
these languages have historic importance, they were taken down
from the shelf, dusted off and allowed to shine in their own right, as
in the almost biblical Latin message, "Greetings to you, whoever
you are: we have good will towards you and bring peace across
space." The Swedish message was personal: "Greetings from a
computer programmer in the little university town of Ithaca, on the
planet Earth." I especially like the Mandarin Chinese greeting; its
casualness reminds me of a postcard to friends—"Hope everyone's
well. We are thinking about you all. Please come here to visit us
when you have time."

A few people asked the extraterrestrials to be in touch, such as   8
the Indian speaking in Gujarati: "Greetings from a human being of
the Earth. Please contact." A fellow Indian speaking in Rajasthani
had other sentiments: "Hello to everyone. We are happy here and
you be happy there." The Turkish speaker made a leap of faith
when he assumed not only that he would be talking to friends, but
that they would be fluent in Turkish: "Dear Turkish-speaking
friends, may the honors of the morning be upon your heads." . . .

Voyager has been compared to a bottle with a note inside tossed   9
over the railing of a ship at sea. It is, though the bottle is custom-
built and the note scribbled in computer instead of pencil. We are
tossing our bottle into the void of the sky. Whether it will ever be
found by someone walking on a galactic beach will not be known
by our generation. Our distant progeny will have this to look forward to.

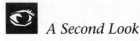 *A Second Look*

1 If there are intelligent extraterrestrials in the distant regions where Voyager travels, it is unlikely that their language will be English or Swedish or one of the many dialects of Indian or Chinese. What is the purpose, then, of sending greetings in fifty-five major languages?

2 In another part of her account, Sagan says that "there were two audiences for whom this message was being prepared—those of us who inhabit Earth, and those who exist on the planets of distant stars." Why should Earth-dwellers be considered an audience for the Voyager messages?

3 Sagan's essay contains several difficult words and some rather complicated sentences. What kind of audience do you think she is aiming at? Can we assume that she is writing especially for readers familiar with the technical vocabulary of space science?

4 It is difficult for the average person to imagine the size of our galaxy, much less the enormous distances of extragalactic space. How does Sagan try to make the hugeness of the Voyager enterprise more understandable?

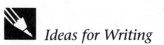 *Ideas for Writing*

Suppose that you had the opportunity to send a brief message to extraterrestrial beings. What would you say? Write a one- or two-paragraph greeting to an audience deep in or even beyond our galaxy. Assume that they can read and interpret your words but that they know little about the Earth and nothing at all about you.

Power from the Sky

Joseph Knapka

Looking Forward

We often assume that growth on Earth is limited by our dwindling resources and that growth beyond our planet is limited by insufficient money and technology. In this student research paper, Joseph Knapka challenges these assumptions and argues that we can cross these frontiers too.

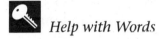 *Help with Words*

biosphere *(paragraph 1):* that area of the Earth's land, water, and atmosphere that can support life

simulation *(paragraph 2):* model

interstellar *(paragraph 5):* among the stars

finite *(paragraph 5):* limited

photovoltaic cells *(paragraph 6):* units that can produce electricity when exposed to light

array *(paragraph 7):* an orderly arrangement

contemplated *(paragraph 7):* considered

alleviate *(paragraph 10):* reduce, lessen

There exists in the world today a school of thought which holds that the resources of man are limited to the resources of the planet on which he evolved—that there is no more living space, energy, or food available to us other than that which we find within the biosphere of Planet Earth. Much of the foundation for this sort of thinking can be found in a slim volume called *The Limits to Growth*, published by a group called the Club of Rome (Heppenheimer, *Future*, 204).

The Club of Rome conducted a study in 1971 that, on the surface, 2 seems to support this line of thought. They designed and executed a computerized simulation of the world's economy, taking into account such variables as pollution, population growth, available energy, food, and standard of living. The results of the simulation showed that the collapse of human civilization worldwide was due within the century (205).

However, the model used for the study neglected some very important relationships. Possibly the best criticism came from Robert Boyd, of the University of California. A year after the *Limits* model was run, Boyd designed a new version. Starting with the same basic model, he added one more variable: technology. He wrote equations which simulated the assumptions that growth of technology could hold resource availability steady, increase standard of living (and hence indirectly decrease population growth[1]), and/or increase the output of agricultural land. His model provided a much more hopeful viewpoint, predicting a leveling-off of population growth, and a worldwide increase in standard of living, well into the next century.[2]

But the question remains: are Boyd's assumptions necessarily 4 any more correct than the Club of Rome's were? There is evidence that, if people act rationally, the answer is definitely "yes."

Consider, for a moment, the sun. With sufficient energy, and 5 means to control it, practically anything can be accomplished, from food synthesis to interstellar flight. Stars are the universe's ultimate energy source, and the human race has a prime specimen right next door. Of course, all energy used today comes from the sun, but only indirectly. Fossil fuels, for instance, are the result of sun-nourished matter being compressed in the crust of the planet. However, fossil fuels are finite resources, and that is one area in which the *Limits to Growth* assumption holds completely true. Sun and Earth cannot replace our fossil fuels as fast as we use them up. The sun itself, however, being much longer-lived, is almost unlimited in the amount of energy it produces. All we need to do to take advantage of that is to figure out a way of utilizing the sun's energy more directly.

Not surprisingly, ways have been thought of to do this. Solar 6 energy has been fairly popular as a home-heating scheme, and photovoltaic cells, or photocells, can be used to convert sunlight directly into electricity. However, these schemes have two problems: the atmosphere, and the planet it surrounds. Cloudless days are rare in most parts of the world, and in any case the Earth's own shadow limits daylight time to a bare 50% of each 24-hour period.

The obvious solution to these problems is to put the photocell 7 array above the atmosphere, which is exactly what is being contemplated. Furthermore, since the zero-gravity orbital environment imposes much less stress on large structures than does the Earth's surface gravity, these photocell arrays can be built on a very large scale—conceivably, one array could have a surface area of hundreds of square kilometers. The array would catch sunlight, convert it to electricity, and beam it to ground stations via microwave transmissions. In tests microwave power transmission has efficiency factors of over 70% (Heppenheimer, *Colonies*, 223). The concept of these solar power satellites (SPS) has been around since 1968, and today we have the technology to make it practical (Heppenheimer, *Suns*, 83).

The price tag is actually fairly modest when one considers that, 8 after the initial investment is paid off, the energy obtained is essentially free. The most promising estimate was a bid by Boeing Corporation, which claimed that it could have a power satellite operational within a decade, at a total expenditure of under $300 billion. Additional satellites would be much cheaper, since the major investments, primarily the satellite construction station, would already be complete (Heppenheimer, *Colonies*, 147).

A single power satellite would have a solar reception area of per- 9 haps ten square kilometers. If the density of solar energy at the Earth's orbit is one watt per square meter, and the photocells convert the solar energy to electricity with 80% efficiency, and the power transmission beam transmits the energy down to the surface with 70% efficiency, then the total energy obtained would be approximately 6,000,000 × .80 × .70 watts, or 3.36 megawatts. This is approximately enough energy to maintain Manhattan Island's electrical supply on a constant basis.

The beauty of the system is that the work force would not need to 10 be large—perhaps five hundred to build the first satellite, although the number would get larger immediately, since it would be necessary to mine the moon and asteroid belts for raw materials. When the population began to expand into space in earnest, huge space stations called O'Niell colonies would be built—essentially self-contained worlds, complete with hills, streams, and cities. They would serve to alleviate much of the population pressure of the homeworld, since a large O'Niell colony could house millions of people. Again, we have the technology today, although not the budget, to build such structures.[3] However, the power satellites would provide us with the financial base needed to colonize space, since we could sell energy to other nations—and man's expansion to the stars could begin.

Notes

[1]When the standard of living of a population rises, its growth rate tends to decrease. This effect causes a decrease in unemployment because of the smaller available work force. These effects were mentioned in *Toward Distant Suns*, but Heppenheimer does not document this information.

[2]This paragraph is summarized from various sections of several of Heppenheimer's works.

[3]This paragraph is summarized from several chapters of Gerard K. O'Niell's *The High Frontier*.

Works Cited

Heppenheimer, T. A. *Colonies in Space*. Harrisburg: Stackpole, 1976.

————. *The Real Future*. New York: Doubleday, 1983.

————. *Toward Distant Suns*. Harrisburg: Stackpole, 1979.

O'Niell, Gerard K. *The High Frontier*. New York: Doubleday, 1982.

 A Second Look

1 In paragraphs 1 and 2, Knapka states an idea with which the rest of his paper disagrees. How does he signal the beginning of his counterargument in paragraph 3? How does he continue his argument in paragraphs 4 and 5?

2 How are the arguments about increasing energy sources and colonizing space related?

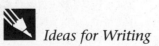 *Ideas for Writing*

1 In paragraph 10, Knapka mentions O'Niell colonies, described as "essentially self-contained worlds, complete with hills, streams, and cities

. . . [which] could house millions of people." Imagine what life in such a colony would be like. What would be the advantages and disadvantages of living there? What would the inhabitants likely miss most when they moved from Earth? In several paragraphs, describe how you think life in an O'Niell colony would be lived, and explain why you would or would not like to try living there.

2 Your instructor may wish you to write a short library paper in which you support your ideas with the ideas of others, just as Knapka does in "Power from the Sky." If so, pick a subject about which you can easily find material in the library. A few suggestions are the effects of TV violence, banning books in public schools, mandatory seat belt laws, vitamin therapy for the common cold, and mandatory drug testing for athletes. Your instructor may suggest other topics.

   When you have picked a topic, check the library for information on it. Try to find several books, articles, or newspaper stories stating different points of view. Combine this material with your own ideas, as Knapka did in his paper.

   Your instructor can give you suggestions for organizing your paper and show you how to give credit to those whose ideas or actual words you are borrowing.

Making Connections

The word *frontier* originally meant a borderland; however, at least in American usage, the definition has grown much broader with time. In the nineteenth century, it often referred to cheap, plentiful land, which was available to those with the strength and courage to tame it. Now the word has come to refer to any area of activity that gives the opportunity for advancement and achievement. Based on the essays in this unit (as well as others in the text that you might want to consider), what would be your extended definition of *frontier*? Can you think of other frontiers besides those in this unit or text?

Acknowledgments

Jack Agueros: "Halfway to Dick and Jane," from *The Immigrant Experience* edited by Thomas Wheeler. Copyright © 1971 by the Dial Press. Reprinted by permission of Doubleday, a division of Bantam Doubleday Dell Publishing Group, Inc.

Maya Angelou: "I Know Why the Caged Bird Sings," from *I Know Why the Caged Bird Sings* by Maya Angelou. Copyright © 1969 by Maya Angelou. Reprinted by permission of Random House, Inc.

Arthur Ashe: "Send Your Children to the Libraries." Copyright © 1977 by The New York Times Company. Reprinted by permission.

Pete Axthelm: "Where Have All the Heroes Gone?" Copyright 1979 by Newsweek, Inc. All rights reserved. Reprinted by permission.

Dave Barry: "Pranks for the Memory," from *Dave Barry Talks Back* by Dave Barry. Copyright © 1991 by Dave Barry. Reprinted by permission of Crown Publishers, Inc.

John C. Bennett: "My First Hunting Trip." Reprinted by permission of John C. Bennett.

Jennifer Bitner: "Women Wasted." This article was reprinted in the second edition by permission of Jennifer Bitner. Permission to reprint must be obtained from the publisher.

Fredric Brown: "The Answer." Copyright © 1954 by Fredric Brown; © renewal 1982 by Elizabeth C. Brown for the Estate of Fredric Brown. Reprinted by permission of Roberta Pryor, Inc.

Rachel Carson: "A Fable for Tomorrow," from *Silent Spring* by Rachel Carson. Copyright © 1952 by Rachel Carson. Copyright renewed 1990 by Roger Christie. Reprinted by permission of Houghton Mifflin Company. All rights reserved.

John R. Coleman: "Blue-Collar Journal: A College President's Sabbatical." Copyright © 1974 by John R. Coleman. Reprinted by permission of Collier Associates.

Barry Commoner: "Making Peace with the Planet," from *Making Peace with the Planet* by Barry Commoner. Copyright © 1975, 1988, 1989, 1990 by Barry Commoner. Reprinted by permission of Pantheon Books, a division of Random House, Inc.

Colette Dowling: "Becoming Helpless" from *The Cinderella Complex*, copyright © 1981 by Colette Dowling. Reprinted by permission of Summit Books, a division of Simon & Schuster, Inc.

Catherine Ettlinger: "Skiing with the Guys." Reprinted with permission from *Working Woman* Magazine. Copyright © 1987 by Working Woman/McCall's Group.

Marjorie Franco: "Yes, Women and Men Can Be 'Just Friends.'" Reprinted from *Today's Health*, May 1975, by special permission. © 1975 Family Media, Inc. All rights reserved.

Robert Peter Gale and Thomas Hauser: "Final Warning," from *Final Warning: The Legacy of Chernobyl* by Robert Peter Gale and Thomas Hauser. Copyright 1988 by Warner Books, Inc. Reprinted by permission.

Edward Goldsmith and Others: "The Balance of Nature," from *Imperiled Planet* by Edward Goldsmith et al. Copyright © 1990 by The MIT Press. Reprinted by permission.

Ellen Goodman: "The Company Man," from *At Large* by Ellen Goodman. Copyright © 1981 by Washington Post Co. Reprinted by permission of Simon & Schuster, Inc.

Steven Graves: "The First Kiss." Reprinted by permission of Steven Graves.

Bob Greene: "Good Morning, Merry Sunshine," from *Good Morning, Merry Sunshine* by Bob Greene. Copyright © 1984 by John Deadline Enterprises, Inc. Reprinted by permission of Atheneum Publishers, an imprint of Macmillan Publishing Company.

Ryan Hardesty: "Up the Hill." Reprinted by permission of Ryan Hardesty.

Langston Hughes: "Salvation," from *The Big Sea* by Langston Hughes. Copyright 1940 by Langston Hughes. Copyright renewed 1968 by Arna Bontemps and George Houston Bass. Reprinted by permission of Hill and Wang (now a division of Farrar, Straus and Giroux, Inc.)

Robert Jastrow: "Our Brain's Successor," from *Science Digest*, March 1981. Reprinted by permission of Robert Jastrow.

Garrison Keillor: "After a Fall." Copyright © 1982 by Garrison Keillor, originally appeared in The New Yorker, from *Happy to Be Here* by Garrison Keillor. Used by permission of Viking Penguin, a division of Penguin Books USA Inc.

Martin Luther King, Jr.: "Stride Toward Freedom," from *Stride Toward Freedom* by Martin Luther King, Jr. Copyright © 1958 by Martin Luther King, Jr. Copyright renewed 1986 by Coretta Scott King, Dexter King, Martin Luther King, III, Yolanda King, and Bernice King. Reprinted by permission of HarperCollins Publishers.

Stephen King: "Head Down," The New Yorker, April 16, 1990. © 1990 Stephen King. Reprinted by permission of The New Yorker.

Maxine Hong Kingston: "The Woman Warrior," from *The Woman Warrior: Memoirs of a Girlhood Among Ghosts* by Maxine Hong Kingston. Copyright © 1975, 1976 by Maxine Hong Kingston. Reprinted by permission of Alfred A. Knopf, Inc.

Joseph Knapka: "Power from the Sky and Other Neat Tricks: The Fallacy of 'Limits to Growth.'" This article was reprinted in the second edition by permission of Joseph Knapka. Permission to reprint must be obtained from the publisher.

Miami Herald: "Ashe's Message Not About AIDS," editorial. Copyright © 1992 The Miami Herald. Reprinted with permission.

Mariah Burton Nelson: "We Are the Best," from *Are We Winning Yet?* by Mariah Burton Nelson. Copyright © 1991 by Mariah Burton Nelson. Reprinted by permission of Random House, Inc.

James A. Perkins: "Chicken Gizzards," from *Billy the Kid, Chicken Gizzards, and Other Tales* by James A. Perkins, Dawn Valley Press, 1977. Reprinted by permission of James A. Perkins.

Kathy M. Ponder: "Straight Talk About Heroes," The Lexington Herald-Leader, January 31, 1992. Reprinted by permission of Kathy M. Ponder.

Laura B. Randolph: "Black Women in the White House," Ebony Magazine, October, 1990. © 1990 Johnson Publishing Co., Inc. Reprinted by permission of Ebony Magazine.

David Raymond: "On Being Seventeen, Bright, and Unable to Read." Copyright © 1976 by The New York Times Company. Reprinted by permission.

Roger Rosenblatt: "Out of Work in America," Life Magazine, August 1991. © 1991 The Time Inc. Magazine Company. Reprinted by permission.

Linda Salzman Sagan: "A Voyager's Greetings," from Carl Sagan et al., *Murmurs of Earth*. Copyright © 1978 by Random House, Inc. Reprinted by permission of the author and the author's agents, Scott Meredith Literary Agency, Inc.

Peggy Say and Peter Knobler: "Forgotten," from *Forgotten: A Sister's Struggle to Save Terry Anderson* by Peggy Say and Peter Knobler. Copyright © 1991 by Peggy Say and Peter Knobler. Reprinted by permission of Simon & Schuster, Inc.

Andrew Shanley: "The Great Sisters and Brothers War," from *Woman's Day,* January 20, 1987. Reprinted by permission of Andrew Shanley.

Anne Barrett Swanson: "Thoughts While Putting on Mascara Before Giving a Keynote Address," from *Voices, Visions & Viewpoints*, Minnesota Women's Press, June, 1991. Copyright © 1991 by Anne Barrett Swanson. Reprinted by permission of the author.

Piri Thomas: "Down These Mean Streets," from *Down These Mean Streets* by Piri Thomas. Copyright © 1967 by Piri Thomas. Reprinted by permission of Alfred A. Knopf, Inc.

John Updike: "Ex-Basketball Player," from *The Carpentered Hen and Other Tame Creatures* by John Updike. Copyright © 1957, 1982 by John Updike. Reprinted by permission of Alfred A. Knopf, Inc.

Kurt Vonnegut, Jr.: "Harrison Bergeron," from *Welcome to the Monkey House* by Kurt Vonnegut, Jr. Copyright © 1961 by Kurt Vonnegut, Jr. Originally published in *Fantasy and Science Fiction*. Reprinted by permission of Doubleday, a division of Bantam Doubleday Dell Publishing Group, Inc.

Angela Waugh: "Two Dads Are Better Than One?" Reprinted by permission of Angela Waugh.

Rick Weiss: "Significant Other," The New York Times, September 1, 1991. Copyright © 1991 by The New York Times Company. Reprinted by permission.

Photo Credits

pp. 2, 50, 120, 170, 194, © Charles Harbutt/Actuality Inc.; p. 22, © Joan Liftin/Actuality Inc.; p. 70, © TOPHAM-PA/The Image Works; p. 98, © Jim Fossett/The Image Works; p. 140, © Jim Mahoney/The Image Works; p. 220, © Phillippe Gontier/The Image Works